MW00510852

Dark Psychology:

The 101 Secrets of the Art of

Reading and Influencing People, How to Stop Being Manipulated, Avoid Mind Control and Learn to use NLP Manipulation Techniques for Social Influence

TABLE OF CONTENTS

2

Introduction

Dark Psychology is one of the arts of persuasion and mind control. Psychology refers to the study of the behaviors of human beings. It is the center of every human being's thinking, their deeds, and socialization. Therefore, Dark Psychology is the phenomenon through which human beings apply manipulation, persuasion, and mind control techniques to fulfill their intentions. In dark psychology, there is the 'Dark Psychology Triad,' which is one of the easiest predictors of manipulator's behavior, collapsed relationships, and also being problematic. The Dark Psychology Triad includes:

• The psychopathy - They are friendly and always charming, impulsive, selfish, lack empathy, and are not remorseful.

• The narcissists - These kinds of people are filled with ego, grandiosity, and have no empathy or sympathy.

•   The Machiavellians - These kinds of people use
manipulation, persuasion, and mind control to exploit and lure
people. In addition to this, they are always immoral.
No one in this world would wish to be a victim of manipulation
even though it happens whether you are conscious or
unconscious of it. In the case you fall under manipulation, it is
not necessarily someone in the Dark Psychology Triad, but you
will face persuasion daily. Manipulation tactics always manifest
themselves in regular commercials, Internet advertisements,
sales tactics, and in your workplaces. If you are a parent, you
must have come across these tactics in your everyday life since
children tend to experiment with tactics so that they can get
what they want. Dark Psychology is used by people who you
genuinely love or trust. In Dark Psychology, the manipulators
use the following tactics:

•   They flood their targets with love, compliments, and
buttering up to acquire what they want.

•   They lie too much, exaggerate things, tell untruths or
even tell partially true stories.

•   They deny their love to those they are targeting through
withholding their attention.

•   They give some choice routes that distract you from the
choice you do not want them to make.

•   They apply reverse Psychology, which involves doing
something which motivates their victim to do the opposite,
which turns out to be what they wanted.

- They use words assumed to have the same definition, but later tell you they meant something else throughout the conversation.

Dark Psychology aims at reminding you how easy it is to get manipulated. You should, therefore, assess your techniques in all areas of your life, workplace, leadership, intimate relationships, and parenting. The people who use these Dark Psychology tactics are aware of what they are doing and manipulate you intentionally to get what they want. Some end up using unethical ways in their manipulative techniques though they are never aware of it. Other people learned their manipulative techniques at a very early age. For instance, if you applied a particular behavior when you were a kid and you got what you wanted, you are more likely to use the same technique every time you want something.

Others are trained or get to know these tactics just by happenstance. The training programs that can prepare you on the ideas and concepts of Dark Psychology and unethical persuasion techniques are mostly the sales and marketing programs. When doing sales or marketing, dark tactics are applied to either create a brand or sell a product that ends up benefiting the sales assistants rather than the customer's needs. You get convinced that using such dark tactics is okay as it helps the buyer. The following are the people who use Dark Psychology tactics the most:

- The Narcissists – Narcissistic people, always have a high sense of self-worth. They want everyone to realize and recognize their superiority. They still want to be adored or worshipped. Therefore, they use dark tactics to manipulate, persuade, or control the minds of their targets.
- The Sociopaths – They are charming, bright, but impulsive. They lack emotions and are remorselessness; hence end up using Dark Psychology tactics to mend relationships with people they can easily take advantage of.
- The Attorneys - Most of the attorneys emphasize on winning their cases such that they opt for dark manipulation tactics to acquire what they want.
- Political Figures – They are always using shady manipulation tactics while campaigning for people to elect them. They use dark psychological techniques to prove to the voters that they are the best and deserve the post they are fighting for.
- Salespeople – The salespeople are always focusing on the benefits rather than the customer's satisfaction. They use dark persuasion tactics to make the buyer buy their products.
- Leaders – They use dark manipulation tactics to have great efforts, submission, and higher performance from their dependents.
- Speakers – Various speakers, especially public speakers, practice dark persuasion tactics to influence their audience.

This helps them sell more products, predominantly in the final stages.

•   The Selfish – Anyone with a hidden agenda of self before others always uses dark manipulation tactics to get what they want first at someone's costs.

Most of Dark Psychology tactics seem to step even on your toes. Speakers and salespeople are everyday users of these dark tactics. You should, therefore, note that, whether working, writing, talking, or making sales, you are neither supposed to use these dark tactics. Various people tend to admit that their professions require them to practice dark tactics, especially if their aim is to maintain the company's top positions or to avoid losing customers.

It is unfortunate because if they fail to exercise these tactics, there will be short-term sales as well as revenue that will ultimately lead to customers not trusting the company, poor business tactics, employees becoming disloyal, and less successful business results. This calls for you to know the difference between motivation and manipulation tactics that are good or dark. This can be achieved if you assess your intents. If a tactic benefits you alone, then it must be an ominous manipulation task.

Chapter 1 History Of Persuasion Aristotle's Three Models Of Persuasion: (Ethos, Pathos, Logos)

Persuasion has a long history, going back to when humans discovered how to use it to our advantage. Persuasion is defined as a type of behavior that is employed as a means to influence someone's way of thinking, beliefs, decisions, motivation, and behavior.

It can be subtle and undetectable, done covertly, or more obvious, such as a form of encouragement.

The reasons for persuasion vary and are commonly used for personal and/or financial gain. It's a method applied throughout history for political and social gain. One notable example is how the Greeks viewed forms of persuasion, as a way to measure the suitability of a politician or position of authority. The ability to persuade was valued highly, and those who were successful were regarded as worthy of election.

Aristotle, a Greek philosopher, regarded persuasion as an essential skill to acquire and develop for a variety of reasons. It can be argued that persuasion, if used in its most skillful form, can deflect a lot of negative attributes and help someone gain favor, regardless of the circumstance. An example of this is a court case, where a defendant or their lawyer can argue their innocence by way of persuasion. Even where a defendant is believed to be guilty, persuasion can (and has) convince a judge or jury that evidence is circumstantial or that a witness's testimony is not credible. There is more to this method than simply convincing an individual or group of a certain belief or concept with a smooth presentation and convincing words; it includes a far more in-depth study and observation of the people who are to be persuaded. Many of these attributes are useful in winning an argument or a case, whether the person employing the persuasion techniques is correct or not. In some cases, it's not about right or wrong, but instead, a variance in opinions or beliefs where persuasion can go a long way to convince people to see the other side of the debate.

What Are The Different Types Of Persuasion?

Rhetoric is a powerful method of persuasion, which involves the careful study and observation of people, either in groups, as individuals or in society, to better understand how best to apply the "art" of persuasion. Observing people would entail a lot of studies, including employing skilled writers, artists, and speakers with the expertise and talent to persuade. A modern example of this method can be seen in advertisements aimed at specific demographics to promote the sale of a product, or a political campaign targeting undecided voters, to sway their decision one way or another.

The goal is not only to get your attention but to maintain it by "speaking" to you in a way that evokes an emotional response or action. This could result in an emotional plea to support one political party instead of others or to purchase a certain product or service because of a certain nostalgia or connection with family or co-workers.

The reasons for using persuasive techniques is not always secretive or malicious: it can be a good way to convince someone to reconsider making the wrong decision that could result in a detrimental outcome, or serve as a form of positive encouragement or reinforcement as a form of empowerment, such as "you can do it" and "what have you got to lose, come on!" When persuasion takes on a more direct tone, it may seem like a strong form of encouragement. While this may work for some people, it doesn't have the same impact on others. Some people thrive on overt persuasion and may otherwise not achieve a milestone or "go for it" without that persuasive push. On the other hand, some people prefer more autonomy and do not respond well. This is where covert or more subtle forms of persuasion can be useful in influencing them.

Recognizing the different signs of persuasion is key to knowing if someone is using these methods on you. It may not be as obvious as coaxing someone to change their mind or try something new. Some forms of persuasion may be subtle and difficult to detect initially.

Understanding the reasons behind persuasive techniques and the different purposes they serve can help determine if you may be on the receiving end and the reasons why.

Three Basic Forms Of Persuasion

There are three types of persuasion: ethos, logos, and pathos, according to Aristotle. Each method appeals to a different source and has its reason for use:

Ethos

Ethos is known as the persuasion using ethics or morality as a basis. In this method of persuasion, the speaker or individual applying this method is trustworthy, credible, and knowledgeable. In their speech or debate, a credible person will make use of their related expertise and knowledge to support their argument. This is done by citing relevant sources and using their credibility as an expert to persuade the listener of their legitimacy.

This method is regarded as respectful in that it doesn't intend to sway the listener for unethical gain or advantage. The speaker's reputation and status carry a lot of weight in terms of credibility, though this can also be established by using carefully constructed arguments that show that they are ethical.

Logos

Logos is based primarily in logic, or the application of logic to reason with or persuade someone. This method involves using evidence and related studies to support an argument. It's a clear, concise form that doesn't convince someone based on pseudo-science or skewed facts, but rather, it appeals to people who are not easily persuaded unless facts and their related sources support the argument. The format of logos is usually presented in a clear, sometimes chronological, and progressive manner to show how a subject or topic began as disputable, followed by studies and observation to gain factual information to support the argument.

Pathos

Pathos is a method of persuasion that uses the emotion of the recipient (the person being persuaded). This is one of the most powerful and frequently used methods of persuasion. Pathos appeals to an audience's emotions, including their passions, imagination, creativity, and sympathetic nature. While the aim of this method is similar to logos and ethos, pathos can become very deceptive is using a vulnerable person's or group's emotions to their advantage. This can be seen in high control groups, where the promise of making lots of money or reaping the rewards of following a set of rules or belief system. Emotional persuasion can also be powerful in helping the audience identify with the speaker and/or their supporters, by sharing personal experiences and anecdotes that can convince people they are sincere and genuine, or "just one of us." The danger with employing pathos is how it can be misused to take advantage of a vulnerable or gullible group of people who are looking for quick answers and solutions to their problems.

Chapter 2 Six Theories On Psychology Of Manipulation

Reciprocation

Give something to get something, right? Remember the story of the chicken who planted grain so that her chicks could eat? She asked for help to sow the grain, to keep the field clean from weeds, to harvest the grain, and finally, to make the bread. She asked her neighbors and friends to help, but in the end, no one was interested until the bread was hot and ready to eat. Since her neighbors had not given her anything in the form of help, she was not inclined to provide them with any of the final product.

That give and take is the first principal of getting along in life, and it's known as one of the foundational principals of persuasion as well. Reciprocity merely means that if you give someone something, they are more likely to provide you with something in return.

Commitment and Consistency

We, humans, have a "reality" surrounding us at all times. I put this "reality" in quotes because it is a reality of our creation. Our brains have an innate ability to tell stories, and we tell ourselves stories all of the time. We tell ourselves stories of the type of person we believe we are and how we behave feeds into that story. When presented with a choice, you make that choice based on the story of who you are. One of the options looks "right" to us because making that choice is consistent with what we believe a person like us would do.

Social Proof

This core persuasion principle is also sometimes referred to as Consensus. Social proof feeds directly from the previous storytelling of Commitment and Consistency. We have told ourselves a story of what we believe we are, what we stand for, and the kind of person we are. To reinforce that story, we look at how other people behave for Social Proof of how people like us should react in a particular situation.

Now more than ever, the Internet has created countless places where we can go for this type of reinforcement. Some of that reinforcement is legitimate, some not so much. All of it is used as a powerful tool for persuasion, as we'll find out going forward.

Authority

Now once we have decided on the type of person we are and we've assembled with the kinds of people we believe reinforce that identity; the next step is to seek out knowledgeable people to reinforce what we've told ourselves to be true. That's where the idea of Authority takes hold.

As sane people, we are likely to take the advice of people who appear to have more knowledge about a subject than we do. That is certainly necessary. No one can know everything, not even with smartphones and Google, just a tap away. We seek out the advice of people who know more about a subject than we do.

We'll talk more about using this in persuasion later.

Liking

Liking is one of those core principles that seem obvious, but yet it needs definition since it is at the hub of all types of persuasion. Liking, simply put, means that you are much more likely to be persuaded by someone that you like.

If you don't like someone, are you going to take their advice? Probably not. We, humans, are wired to make snap judgments about almost every situation we get into, and one of the most straightforward decisions to make is whether we like someone or not. Every person you meet triggers a feeling instantly of comfort or wariness. This was a survival skill in the early days of our evolution, and it still holds sway today, as we'll see.

Scarcity

Speaking of evolution's early days, our final persuasion principle is an obvious holdover from the early days of staying alive. Scarcity makes things more valuable to us, so when something seems like it is limited in quantity, we are more likely to want it.

Sand is commonplace; gold is not. Which would you rather have? Or more to the point, what does all humankind want more? It most certainly used to be food that was so valuable, so that early man found ways to preserve food when it was abundant so that it would be around when food got scarce.

17

Survival depends on specific resources that can be in short supply, so humans are naturally prone to try and save and hang on to that which is not always available. Since this is core hardwiring in our brains, we'll see that this is an often-used method of persuasion today.

Chapter 3 Character Traits Of Manipulator (Common Traits)

Most of us might have experienced emotional manipulation at some point or another. It is quite useful and is the main reason why unscrupulous individuals like emotional predators use it so often. In 2012, Facebook conducted a secret experiment in conjunction with several researchers from the University of California and Cornell. In this experiment that lasted for a week, the researchers manipulated the content viewed by over 700,000 Facebook users. The intentional manipulation of the feed viewed by the targeted Facebook users was such that a portion of them considered only negative stories, while others saw several positive ones. At the end of the week, the posts made by the users whose feed was riddled with negative posts posted harmful content themselves. So, the research conclusively proves that the mood of an individual can be influenced based on the content shown. Since the prior approval of the users was not obtained, this experiment drew severe backlash on a global scale (Segelken, H.G., Shackford, S., 2014).

One of the scariest aspects of this faux pas made by Facebook was how easily the emotions of a person could be manipulated. After all, by merely tweaking one's newsfeed, Facebook managed to control their emotions. If it is this easy to manipulate someone, then how easy can it be for real, live individuals to manipulate you? It shows how easy it is to shape one's psyche.

The knowledge of your weaknesses and triggers in the hands of an emotional predator can effectively destroy your self-worth and even make you question your sanity. This is one of the reasons why emotional manipulation is destructive. You cannot regain control of your life if you don't fight off the manipulative tactics used by others. In this section, you will be given information about how you can spot manipulation. Once you are aware of what to look for, it becomes easier to take corrective action.

Emotional manipulators will undermine your grasp of reality quite quickly. They will do this by using their skillful lying techniques. They might insist that something didn't happen, even when it did. They will change the narration of facts to suit their needs and according to their convenience. The emotional manipulator is so good at lying that you will eventually start to question your reality and start doubting your judgment. By insisting that it is all in your mind and it is a figment of your overactive imagination, the manipulators will get out of any trouble quickly.

Emotional manipulators display a lot of inconsistencies in both their words and actions. They might tell you one thing, but their efforts might convey something else altogether. The emotional manipulator might promise to do something. Then when the time comes to follow through, they can quickly disavow any promises made and even claim that you are unreasonable. Initially, a manipulator might tell you how lucky he is to have found you and then start acting like you are a burden all of a sudden. By doing this, he is effectively undermining your selfworth and making you question your behavior. The manipulator is trying to mold your perception to suit his needs and wants. An emotional manipulator is quite adept at using the guilt of his victims to his advantage. For instance, if you ever bring up any issue or problem you have with the manipulator's behavior, he will make you feel guilty for even thinking that way. He will shift all the guilt onto you and also victimize himself to disengage any potential confrontation. On the other hand, if you don't share your issues or talk about any problems you're having, he will once again blame you for being distant and keeping it all to yourself. While dealing with an emotional manipulator, keep in mind that he will never allow you to be right about anything. Regardless of what you do, you will always be wrong, and he will always be correct. If you ever have a problem with the relationship, he will suggest that it is all because of you. In any relationship, if you feel like you can never win or never be right, it is quite likely that you are dealing with an emotional manipulator.

Emotional manipulators love to victimize themselves. The best way to shrug off any responsibility is by playing the role of a victim. Regardless of what they do or not do, it will always be someone else's fault except his own. Usually that someone will be you. For instance, if you get upset about something or are angry, then it is your fault; after all, you're the one who had unreasonable expectations. Now, if the manipulator gets angry, then once again, it is because of something you did. Regardless of what happens, it will always be your fault, and you will be the only one accountable for it as well. The emotional manipulator will never take any accountability whatsoever. However, if anything good does happen, the credit flows to them, and anything wrong will always be on you.

Emotional manipulators always seem to be in a hurry, and they tend to skip a couple of steps regardless of whether it is a personal or professional relationship. Too much and too soon seems to be their motto. Not just their slogan, but they also expect the same from you. Any vulnerability or sensitivity portrayed by the manipulator is just a façade. The manipulator uses this tactic to make his victims feel special for being allowed into their inner circle. Not just that, it is also a technique to obtain his victim's sympathy. So, you will not only sympathize with the abuser but will even start accepting any blame doled out to you.

An emotional manipulator is like an emotional black hole. Regardless of what the emotional manipulator feels, he can successfully make everyone else around him feel the same. If he is in a bad mood, then he will ensure that everyone around him feels the same. Well, the worst is yet to come- he will not only make others become aware of his bad mood but will also ensure they feel it. By doing this, he is essentially making others feel responsible for his mood. Once again, this is all about shifting the blame onto others and shrugging off all responsibility. If you feel like you are perpetually under an obligation to fix all the problems in a relationship while your partner does nothing, then you are the victim of emotional abuse and manipulation. They might seem quite eager to help and even volunteer to help, and then when the time comes to keep their word, they will quickly backtrack. The initial eagerness expressed by them swiftly and rapidly turns into sighs and groans of discontent. Their desire to help will go away, and they will start behaving like it is all a massive burden to them. By chance, if you call out this behavior, it will somehow become your fault. Don't be surprised if the manipulator starts telling you that he will still help you and that you are the one who is acting crazy and is being paranoid. What is the goal of all this? Well, it will make you feel like you are indebted to the manipulator and to make you feel guilty. It gives the manipulator a certain degree of control over you.

Regardless of the problems you're facing, the emotional manipulator will always have it worse. Well, at least according to them. They will always try to one-up you. If you complain about a problem, the emotional manipulator will quickly point out that he has it worse, and you must not complain. Are you wondering why they do this? It is to minimize the intensity of your problems to shift the focus onto their pressing issues. It is also done to make their victims feel like they are complaining for no reason. A manipulator cannot stand it when others take away attention from him. The inherent traits of narcissism embedded into the manipulator's psyche make him continuously crave for attention. He will feel threatened when others start getting this attention. To fix this situation, they will come up with tragic stories.

Emotional manipulators are well aware of the strengths and weaknesses of their victims. They will use both these traits against the victim. Once you start opening up to an emotional manipulator, he will quickly use all the knowledge he has about you against you. For instance, if you have any insecurity about your weight or struggle with your body image, the manipulator will use this information against you. He might even make comments about the food you eat, or the way your clothes fit you. He might also start using this information in public to belittle you and gain control over you. The awareness that emotional manipulators have about their victim's thought processes is off the charts.

If you notice any of the signs discussed in this section, you are in a relationship with a manipulator.

Chapter 4 Victims Of Manipulation

Just as predators have several traits, they often all have, so to do their targets. The people that predators choose to target are typically chosen methodically, seeking out those who are least likely to rebel or try to fight back from any sort of manipulation. They can identify potential targets at a glance, needing little more than seconds to pass judgment on whether that person should be pursued with shocking accuracy. They can tell based off of body language, clothing, situations, interactions, and more, who will be able to serve them best, and they frequently act upon it. Here are some of the most common traits people who find themselves victims of manipulators often have.

Lacking Confidence

Due to lacking confidence, an individual can be quite easy to steamroll. Looking for body language that marks someone as lacking confidence is a surefire way for predators to identify an easy target. Those who lack confidence are not likely to put up any sort of fight, either if you attack physically or emotionally. In lacking confidence, the predator can be sure that the individual also requires the ability to defend boundaries or him or herself. When someone comes across as self-confident, he or she exudes an air of someone not as willing to put up with any sort of manipulation without a fight. Those with confidence will fight back when they feel wronged, violated, or hurt, and would have no qualms walking away from a relationship because they trust their judgment.

By seeking someone lacking confidence, a predator goes after the easiest possible target to get whatever is desired, whether it is physical affection, arm candy, money, a home, a sale, a vote, or even just the feeling of having dominated someone else. The predator is able to boost his or her ego through completely taking over another person's life and making decisions for the person. They may want someone around that will always defer to them, allowing them a position of power, even if it is undeserved or unwarranted. They may want someone to make them feel better about themselves, and someone with low selfconfidence is likely to do that.

Sometimes, however, predators will go out of their way to identify someone with higher levels of confidence, as they see it as a game. They make it a challenge to so thoroughly break someone with high confidence that the target allows them to dominate the situation. This predator is doing nothing more than toying with the target and seeks nothing but selfgratification from doing so.

Have Something Desirable

Sometimes, personality has nothing to do with being targets. Sometimes, predators go after someone because they have something the predator wants. Whether it is money, status, a relationship, or anything else, the predator may choose to go after that person in hopes of getting it by association. If the person is someone powerful or influential, the predator may weasel her way into a friendship with the sole intention of pulling from that person's influence in the future. By winning what the other person perceives as a friendship, the manipulator creates an arsenal of people with a wide range of skills, abilities, and prestige that can be used when the need arises. If she wants a new job, she may be able to get a friend to pull strings and get her one, for example.

If what she desires is money, she may worm her way into a friendship or relationship with someone that has a lot of money in an attempt to attract that kind of lifestyle. If her boyfriend is wealthy, he would likely have little issue spending money on her. Further, she may feel as though associating herself with people who have what she wants will help her learn how to achieve what the other people have. Through learning what people are doing and how they are doing it, she may be able to emulate those behaviors in hopes of getting what she wants.

Caregiver-type

Some people are more prone to being caregivers than others. People who are compassionate can become easily manipulated because they seek to believe the best in others and seek to ensure that others' needs are met as thoroughly as possible. The caregiver-type person is likely to see the manipulator and all of his or her flaws but proceed with a relationship anyway, believing that all that is needed to remedy the situation is love and patience. Unfortunately, that resilience to make sure that the manipulator is cared for and nurtured back to mental health also makes the caregiver an easy victim as well.

Because the caregiver is willing to take all of that negative behavior as signs that the manipulator needs more help, he or she will often completely overlook the warning signs and endure the manipulation, feeling as though it will stop eventually. Unfortunately, no amount of love or patience is going to change who someone is, and they are likely to be disappointed as the manipulative behaviors continue to grow, eventually beginning to drain on even the caregiver, whose personality type is prone to patience and resilience.

This is yet another common target for the manipulator because he or she can get away with far worse behavior far quicker than imagined. Because the manipulator knows that very little done will successfully push the caregiver away due to the caregiver's own inherent desire to fix the manipulator, the parasitic manipulator can continue to draw upon the caregiver's goodwill to get anything desired with few repercussions.

Empathetic

Considering that most of the manipulators you will encounter either lack empathy or know how to turn off their empathy to steel themselves from other people's emotional states, it should come as no surprise that they are naturally drawn toward the empathetic.

Empathy is the ability to sense and understand how someone else is feeling. It is as if you have taken yourself and placed yourself in the other person's shoes, understanding exactly how they feel because you know how you would feel in their situation. This sense of putting yourself in someone else's shoes enables humans to ensure that those within their family or tribal unit are taken care of. It extends to other people as well, and those who are particularly empathetic find themselves identifying with other people. They may see the manipulator and decide that they see a person who is clearly in dire need of love and attention. They see the manipulator's flaws and want to try to fix them because they understand how lonely or down, they would feel if they lacked confidence, lacked friends and family, or lacked whatever else it is that they believe the manipulator may be lacking.

The empathetic individual, like the caregiver, will take more than his or her fair share of abuse, justifying it as the manipulator being in a bad situation and that any rational person who had suffered the same way would behave similarly. The empathetic target is also far more susceptible to mind games relating to emotions and guilt trips, and the empathetic nature of the individual is eventually used as a weapon against him- or herself.

Dysfunctional Upbringing

People who have grown up in dysfunction have the disadvantage of never learning what normal, functioning, healthy relationships entail. They typically associate their upbringing with what is normal and seek to replicate those sorts of relationships in adulthood. If a child grew up around parents who fought and argued all the time, with the mother always giving up what she wanted while the father took endlessly, the newfound adult is going to attempt to replicate that dynamic in any adult relationship.

Likewise, someone who grew up in dysfunction is not likely to understand how to set normal or healthy boundaries or how to enforce those boundaries. They will be easily steamrolled, especially if boundaries being disrespected were a common theme growing up. This leaves the individual quite vulnerable, as he has no sense of normalcy and no sense of how to protect himself within a relationship. He does not understand that relationships are supposed to be symbiotic, and because of that, he is far more likely to deal with misbehaviors and abuse from a manipulator.

Knowing this, manipulators look for those who grew up in dysfunction. They are seen as easy targets. Their lack of boundaries makes them easier to manipulate, and their lack of confidence or sense of what a healthy relationship looks like means that the target is not likely to see red flags when the manipulative behaviors begin cropping up. With red flags unseen, the manipulation is not seen as a warning sign that the relationship is unhealthy or should be ended. Particularly if abuse and manipulation were prevalent in childhood, the target may have a high tolerance for such behaviors, meaning the predator can escalate quickly and more effectively.

How to identify yourself as the Victim of Covert Manipulation

No one likes being manipulated. When manipulation occurs, you lose your power and your will. You must do what the other person wants. You often have no idea what the other person is planning, and you have no say in the situation. This makes life very difficult, and it can cause you to do things that you don't want to do.

Now that you know the secrets to covert manipulation, you also know what to watch out for. You can reverse the techniques in this book to see when others are manipulating you. You can also flip these tactics on people and give them the manipulation that they are trying to run on you. There are various ways that you can protect yourself against manipulators.

Identify when You are a Victim

Everyone has a gut instinct that rears up when they are used or misguided. Your gut instinct is very sound. You will know when you are a victim. The problem is, a lot of people ignore their instincts. You might ignore yours. You might think something like, "I'm just paranoid" or "What could go wrong if I hang out with this person?" You might think that the harm will be worth the benefits that you could get from knowing this person who gives you bad vibes. Maybe everyone else likes this guy, do you think that you are just weird, and you should like him too. Or maybe he is able to charm you and convince you that he is not so bad, and over time you start to get over your initial bad vibes.

But vibes are not something that you should ever ignore. The minute your gut warns you about someone, listen. Your first impression of someone is never wrong. If you get a terrible first impression, don't give the person a second chance. You know more about someone by just glancing at them than you would think. The human brain is amazingly powerful; you only are conscious of roughly ten percent of your mind, so a lot is going on under the surface that you are not consciously aware of. Your brain is capable of reading people and determining the future far more than you realize.

So, when you get that gut feeling, understand that your brain is working very hard and noticing things that you are not consciously aware of. The person that you get bad vibes may not be matching his body language to his words, or he may be acting oddly in ways that you can't detect easily. Listen to your gut!   If you are just not in touch with your gut at all, or if you have doubts about someone, you might want to consider looking at some other signs. You can identify a manipulator based on his actions and language choices. You can also tell by how you feel around this person. Various clues point out who someone is and what his intentions are.

What Makes You Vulnerable

You may wonder why manipulators are attracted to you, especially if you have had multiple encounters with manipulative types. You may also wonder what you should change about yourself to avoid running into a manipulator in the future.

One thing that makes you vulnerable is being accepted to manipulative treatment and emotional abuse. If you were emotionally abused or repressed as a child, this type of treatment might seem normal to you. You don't know anything else. You don't know how a healthy relationship is supposed to feel. So, you accept the terrible treatment that others would not think of accepting. As a result, you are projecting a sense of vulnerability that draws manipulators from far away. The minute you begin to tolerate their treatment and keep them in your life, they gain power over you and choose to continue using you until they get what they want. Work on increasing your selfesteem and avoiding familiar patterns. If you get that eerie sense of déjà vu when you meet someone, you might want to avoid that person because he is probably reminding you of previous abusive patterns that you have been in.

Another thing that may make you vulnerable is neediness or weakness. If you are in a vulnerable time in life, you might be more open to manipulators. Manipulators can see that you are in need, and they see it as an opportunity to offer you what you need in exchange for what they want. They will use any opportunity to gain control over you, and when you are in a bad period of life, you hand them opportunities. You need to guard your heart and mind, especially well when you are at a disadvantage. Be wary of extremely kind strangers or lifesavers.

Not all heroes are good guys. Your heroes may help you, but they may have hidden intentions. Most people won't do something for free, so watch out.

You may also be a target for manipulation if you have low selfesteem. Events in your life or your childhood may have stripped away from your self-esteem and confidence. You may be emotionally vulnerable. So, you want people who build up your ego. Manipulators can spot this, and they will move in on you, working hard to please you and make you smile. They see a way into your mind through your bruised ego. Try to build your selfesteem by yourself and work on loving yourself.

Signs of a Manipulator

A manipulator is often incredibly superficial. This means that he looks good on the outside, but there is nothing to follow it up on the inside. He is shallow and lacks depth. Everything he does and says is fake, part of a façade that he erects to fool you. So, beware of people who are incredibly charming and attractive when you first meet them. Get to know them before you start confiding in them or trusting them. Don't make a commitment or business deal until you are sure of yourself.

Another sign of a manipulator is that you feel compelled to confide in him or to do what he wants. You always find yourself saying yes when you want to say no. It's impossible to be yourself and to stand up for yourself. He has some sort of power over you that you can't resist. Unfortunately, this power is just a carefully woven web of manipulation, deception, and emotional harm. He will dump you the minute he gets all that he can from you, so don't stick around or make the mistake of thinking that this relationship will last. He does not care, no matter how well he pretends to. Get away from him before the relationship gets too harmful, and he ruins your life.

You may also find yourself saying sorry all of the time. Your guilt eats you up. Every situation with this person seems like your fault. Even if he is at fault, he manages to twist things around so that you feel guilty. He will never take responsibility for anything that he does, and he will always put everything on you. He can do what he wants, but he holds you to exacting standards and punishes you when you don't follow suit. He kills your selfesteem and causes you to hate yourself.

Finally, a manipulator is great at changing your mind. You might feel one way, but after talking with him, you feel a completely different way. He can change your mind and your way of thinking. Sometimes this may even be a good thing, as he makes you think more constructively or positively. But be wary of someone who has so much power over your moods and your thoughts.

Chapter 5 Tips For Dealing With Manipulative People

The first and most important thing that you need to do to defend yourself against mind and emotional control and manipulation is to accept the fact that the person you are dealing with is controlling and manipulative, and that's his or her nature. The reason people stay with controlling individuals is that they operate under the misconception that such people can change. Many controlling and manipulative people tend to have dark personality traits such as narcissism, Machiavellianism, sadism, or psychopathy. That means that the need to control others is just part of who they are.

If you start dating someone (or associating with them in any other way) and you realize that they are controlling, don't delude yourself into thinking that you will be able to change them and make them less controlling. That is part of the manipulation; they'll put out signals that indicate to you that they might be open to change, but that only makes you feel more invested in the relationship. It makes you susceptible to further manipulation and control.

Controlling people won't change on their own; they need to control others is primal, and it's not something that can be easily trained out of a person. So, once you see any of the signs of control that we discussed in the previous chapter, it's time for you to either sever your connection with the person or if he or she is a permanent part of your life (like a family member that you can't completely avoid), you should start considering some of the defensive strategies that we will discuss in this chapter. Once you have accepted that controlling people won't change on their own, it's time to come up with a strategy to deal with them. Towards that end, the first thing you need to do is ensure that you understand all your fundamental human rights, and make sure that the controlling person doesn't violate them. You have every right to stand up and to defend your fundamental rights including the right to be treated with respect; the right to set and pursue your own priorities; the right to express your own needs and feelings; the right to say "NO" to someone's request without feeling guilty about it; the right to have an opinion that differs from that of anyone and everyone else; the right to pursue a happy and healthy life; and the right to protect yourself from threats (including physical, mental, and emotional threats).

If someone infringes on any of these rights, you have a right to act. Controlling people will try to convince you otherwise. They'll tell you don't feel how you feel, or that they didn't mean something the way you interpreted it, but don't ever substitute your own objective judgment for someone else's; if you feel what the manipulator is doing is harmful to you, don't give them the chance to convince you otherwise, because no matter how smart you are, good manipulators will be able to talk you out of anything.

Think of the rights we have listed above as boundaries. Picture them as lines that separate you from everyone else, even the people you love. No one gets to cross those lines. Anyone who does is out to control you; we are not trying to get you to be paranoid, we are trying to get you to be vigilant. It's only by being vigilant that you will be able to see a controlling person come from a mile away, and you'll be able to strategize and to defend yourself.

You need to learn to tune into your real feelings in every situation that you find yourself in. The thing about controlling people is that they try their best to be subtle so that their manipulation techniques can fly under the radar. That means that if you are interacting with such people. At the same time, you are on autopilot, and it can be extremely difficult for you even to recognize the fact that they are trying to control you, so you won't be able to take defensive action.

Whenever anyone makes you have negative feelings, or they make you doubt your conviction about something, it's time to snap out of autopilot mode and tune in to the way you genuinely feel. Define the feeling. Is it guilt? Is it insecurity? Is it selfdoubt? If you feel obligated to act a certain way, try to uncover the reason behind that sense of obligation: Are you afraid? Are you ashamed? Are you reciprocating? Unless you articulate your thoughts and feelings in such moments, you will be unable to tell when you are being manipulated.

Once you get the sense that you are being manipulated or someone is trying to control you, start scrutinizing everything they do. Manipulators work tirelessly to get you to fall into their trap. Every action they take will be tactfully selected to steer you one way or the other. The only way to avoid falling into their trap is by assuming that everything that they put on your path is a potential trap.

Since you know they are controlling, if they do something nice for you, try to identify the ulterior motive in their niceness. If they are mean to you, try to understand the objective behind their meanness. If you see they are trying to bait you into reacting in a specific way, avoid giving them the satisfaction. People who are controlling like to pick soft targets, so if they see that the strategies, they are deploying in the early stages of your association with them aren't working the way they are intended to, the manipulators might leave you alone and find someone else to target. If you don't seem to be malleable in any way, they'll won't want to waste their time on you.

You might also want to start keeping a record of all your interactions with manipulative people. This might seem excessive, but psychologists have long understood that writing things down (or keeping a journal) can help us make sense of the way we feel, and it can help put things into the right perspective.

Several manipulation tactics work because the victim stops believing in their sense of right and wrong, and they stop trusting their perceptions. When you write things down (preferably in an electronic journal), you can always refer back to it, and this will help ensure that you remain grounded in reality.

In cases of gas-lighting, manipulators can convince their victims that things didn't happen the way they remember. In instances of brainwashing, they can satisfy their victims that their feelings about certain past events aren't warranted, or that the memories they have are somehow warped. By keeping a journal, you'll have contemporaneous evidence of the things that happened and the way that you felt at the moment. This means that even if your memories fail you latter own, you will have a way of knowing the truth, and you'll, therefore, be less likely to let the controlling person convince you that you are wrong. You can use either a physical journal or an electric one, but you have to make sure that the controlling person is unable to get his or her hands on it. Some people even use voice recording devices to keep records of their thoughts and emotions. Whatever method you choose, you should preserve and protect your version of events because controlling people won't hesitate to rewrite your history.

You should also try to stay away from manipulative and controlling people. When you meet people for the first time, try to read their body language and their verbal cues, and try to figure out if they have ulterior motives. You can learn to read body language to help you detect when people are cunning or deceptive, but even without any training, you can learn to listen to your instincts about people and to trust those instincts. Psychologists have established that the human mind can be able to accurately perceive potential threats within a few minutes of interacting with someone; try to differentiate between your instinctual reactions to a person and any prejudicial reactions or cognitive biases that you may have about certain demographics.

As we have mentioned several times in this book, manipulative people can come across as charming and charismatic, so, try to look past the superficial charm when you meet a person for the first time.

If the controlling person is a member of your family and you can't completely avoid them, try to keep your interactions to a bare minimum. Avoid spending time with them unless you have to, and avoid situations where you may find yourself alone with them.

If it's a college at work, you should try to steer away from them too, but make sure that your defensive action doesn't hurt your career. If the person is your boss, you might want to think about the long-term implications of working for a person like that.

However, you can try to remain professional and to remind them to do the same whenever they cross the boundary and try to make things personal.

You can also deal with controlling people by calling them out and letting them know that you understand what they are doing.

If you notice that someone is trying to manipulate you in a specific way, confront him, and tell him everything about his plan.

After reading this book, you understand the various tricks that manipulative and controlling people tend to use, so you may be able to identify what someone who is targeting you is trying to do. The next time they are up to their shenanigans, call them out on it. They may react in one of several ways. They may deny it and accuse you of being paranoid. They may fake outrage and try to guilt-trip you for making such serious accusations. They may react in anger since they know that their plan has been unraveled.

Whatever reaction the manipulator throws your way, you have to understand one thing; you are calling them out, not bargaining with them. So, if they try to convince you that you are wrong, just say something like "If you say so" and get away from them. Some of them will leave you and target someone else because they understand that you are too smart for their machinations.

However, others (especially the most malicious of the bunch) may try to retaliate against you with personal attacks, or they may switch strategies and try a different approach altogether. When they do this, call them out on that as well.

Sooner or later, even the more stubborn amongst them will start to realize that they aren't making any headway with you, and they may give up. Few may take each instance of being called out as a challenge to step up their game; try to sever your connection with such people, or you can try calling them out in front of witnesses and warning them to stay away from you. Again, as we've said, manipulative and controlling people tend to gravitate towards easy targets, so if you keep proving that you are no easy target, they'll recognize that they are wasting their effort.

You should also avoid getting emotionally attached to people who you suspect of being controlling. We acknowledge that this is easier said and done. Meeting new people isn't easy, so when you meet someone, you think you might be compatible with. You notice that they have certain traits that could indicate that they are controlling, it's still tempting to give them the benefit of the doubt, because deep within, we want to believe that people are good.

You might decide to indulge someone for a while before you fully understand his or her true nature, but as you do that, you become emotionally linked to them. You fall for their charming behavior, and before you gather enough evidence to prove to yourself that they are controlling conclusively, you would already be too emotionally invested in that relationships just to sever ties with them.

This can be compounded by the flawed thinking that we might be able to change people (which we discussed earlier). The best approach for you is to set your boundaries from day one before you become emotionally invested.

Even if you want to give the person the benefit of the doubt and to get to know them better, you should go into it while understanding your own rules, and don't let emotions cloud that understanding. Stay cordially civil whenever you interact with them (or anyone for that matter), and break with them as soon as you are sure that they are indeed as manipulative as you suspected.

So far, we have looked at how you can defend against mind and emotional control when you discover it early enough before you become too invested in a relationship. However, the fact is that even if you are vigilant, some people will fly under your radar, and they'll get close to you before you notice that they are manipulative. In other cases, you may not have a choice on whether or not such people are in your life; you may be able to choose your romantic partner, but you can't choose your family members, colleagues at work, or your casual acquaintances. So, how do you defend against control in such cases? Well, you may be able to defend yourself by following this simple 3 step process:

Know What You Want

Manipulative people will seek to control you because they want something from you. They want something very specific from you, and they are manipulating or controlling you to increase their chances of getting that thing out of you. The problem is that if you are the kind of person who spends his or her time giving other people what they want, you will waste your whole life serving other people's interests, and you won't ever get what you want out of life. So, no matter how long you have been under the influence of a manipulative person, this is how you have to start; by figuring out what it is that you want. You have to do this as empirically and as systematically as possible. Take a notepad or some kind of writing material, and start evaluating the things that you consider to be your core values. Write down the things in your life that you believe are the most important to you. Is it your family? Your job? Your faith? Your academic pursuits? Certain hobbies you enjoy? A certain person you love? Be honest with yourself and create a list. First, write down whatever comes to mind. The first list will be in random order.

After you have put down all the things that you value, it's time for you to rank them according to how much you prioritize each one of them. List them, from what's most important to what's least important. Don't have any qualm or guilt about the way you rank your values (for example, if you feel your hobby is more important than your career, be honest with yourself in your rankings).

Once you have ranked your values, it's time for you to ask yourself why those values are important to you, and why each value is more important or less important relative to the other things in your list. Try to see if there are any things that you currently value, which may be on your list as a result of the machinations of a controlling person.

If there is a value that seems particularly important to you, or it seems to rank higher than it logically should, it could be up there because someone manipulative drilled it into you over a long period of time. If something that is logically important doesn't rank as highly as it should, it could be that a controlling person has been influencing you to think of it as unimportant. You should also repeat the same exercise, and this time, instead of listing and ranking your values, you should list and rank your favorite ways to spend your free time. Start by listing all the activities that you believe you would like to do when you have the time. In this initial list, don't think practically; think imaginatively. If you had the time, and you had no constraints, no one to hold you back, what would you do?

You should then create a different list, not one of the activities you would lie to do, but one of all the activities that you remember doing during your personal time lately (all the time you spend outside work is technically person time). Rank those activities based on how much time you have spent on them in the past few months.

Now, compare those two lists and spot any differences. What would you like to do that you don't have the time to do? Why don't you have the time to do it? What takes up all your time? Look at the things that you often do, particularly those that take up most of your time. Why do you do those things? Do you truly enjoy doing them, or do you do them out of a sense of obligation? How much "me time" do you really get?

The reason why it's important to assess both your values and the way you spend your time is that someone may have taken over your life, and he may have installed his or her interests at the helm of all your lists.

A controlling person may have destroyed your real values, and he may have forced his values on you. A controlling person may be taking up all your time so that instead of doing what makes you happy, you are spending every free moment you have doing what makes him happy.

If you find yourself spending every evening in a sports bar with your boyfriend when you would rather be taking a dancing class, it means that he has taken control over your evenings and that his leisure activities are a bigger priority for you than your preferred leisure activities. If you find that most of your values are external rather than internal, it means that you care more about someone else's happiness than your own.

Compare how things should be and how they are; if you find that your priorities are not your own, it's time to make a change.

Stand Your Ground

Relationships (whether they are partnerships, marriages, friendships, or workplace relationships), are all about give-andtake. Controlling people and manipulators want to take more than they give or even more than you are willing to give. There is only one way to truly regain control if you are under the influence of a manipulative person, and that is to stand up to them.

Now that you know what you want, and you are able to identify areas in your life where you have compromised too much, and given control over to someone else, you'll have to confront the manipulative people in your life; there are no two ways about it.

It's either you regain control, or you let them control you. To stand up for yourself, you have to reinstate your real value and get rid of the values that have been imposed on you by manipulative people. If, when assessing your values, you realized that you don't have your priorities straight, it's time to let the people who take up your time know that from this point moving on, you will prioritize your interests and their interests will take the back seat.

You have to make it clear to yourself and the people in your life that you have the same rights as they do, and you will no longer let them trample on those rights. Controlling people like to think that they are superior to the people they seek to control, so if you have one in your life right now, he or she is overdue for a reality check.

That's not to say that you should unload on such people, and release all your pent-up anger onto them. You want to make it clear, and in the most logical of terms, that you will no longer be their doormat, that you won't be subservient to them, and that you do, have the moral high ground in that situation.

Here are crucial tips that will help you stand up for yourself:

Realize That No One Else Can Invalidate You

The reason we are so afraid to stand up to controlling people is that we seek external validation. However, the whole concept of external validation is a fallacy. Sure, people can validate us; a boss can praise you in public, a spouse can tell others what a nice person you are, etc. when these people validate us, it only works if we choose to internalize that validation.

The same goes for invalidation. The only reason people have the power to invalidate us is we give them that power; we choose to internalize the invalidation. So, if you are afraid to stand up to someone because you think they'll invalidate you, that's selfsabotage.

No matter what others say, the decision to perceive your thoughts, feelings, and actions as invalid only lies within you. This knowledge should empower you to stand up to anyone, even if you know there's going to be some backlash.

Make People Respect And Value Your Time

Your time on this planet is very short, and it's extremely valuable. As part of standing up for yourself, you have to make sure that the people in your life realize that. If someone shows no respect for your time, then you have to cut the amount of time you give to them.

Ensure That You Always Stay Calm When You Confront Manipulators

You'll come up with a strategy to assert for yourself, but no matter how well thought out your plan is, it could fail if you let emotions get in the way. The only way to win is by staying calm. When you confront a controlling person, make sure that you process the entire interaction through the logical part of your brain, not the emotional part.

This is going to be difficult; as we have already mentioned in the book, emotions are more primal than logic, so it's very easy for them to take over. You have to make a concerted effort to stay calm and logical.

When you stand up to someone, emotion is your enemy; it doesn't matter if it's a positive emotion or a negative one; it's going to work against you. When controlling people see that you are finally standing up to them, they'll react in an emotional way.

Emotions can be infectious (for example, when someone raises their voice in a conversation, you will instinctively do the same). Still, you have to make a mental effort not to mirror the manipulators' emotions. Make your point in a calm voice, and if they react with anger, let them vent, then reiterate your point calmly as you address any points they may have raised in their angry tirade.

You may feel strong emotions in the process, and you'll be tempted to act on those emotions, but at that moment, you should realize that the stakes are much higher than that; you are trying to regain control over your life, and emotions are of no use for you at that moment. Unless you control your emotions, you won't be able to regain control over your life.

Chapter 6 The Goals of Manipulation

Hidden in Minds, Shown in Actions

Manipulators always have their reasons for whatever manipulative behaviors are exhibited, some of which are enumerated below:

Fear: It will surprise you to know that fear drives people to want to be manipulative or to exhibit manipulative traits. The fear that a loved one might leave the manipulator in question could be the reason why a manipulator keeps putting up manipulative characteristics to get the person to stay by them. Fear drives a lot of people into doing different things. A worker could be manipulative for fear of being demoted or fired. A child is likely to engage in manipulation if he's afraid his parents may not give him what he wants.

Ego: Man's ego most times drives him to do whatever he does even when its subconscious or unconscious. So, in the case of manipulation, to protect one's ego, one might need to manipulate his victims into believing he (the manipulator) is never wrong or manipulating the victim into always being the one to apologize. Gaslighting is one technique egoistic manipulators use on their victims by trying to erase whatever their fault in the equation is and quickly turning tables around, making the victim doubt his stance or (in serious cases) sanity. As a man in an effort to protect his ego and dignity and cover his faults or inadequacies from others, he needs to manipulate them.

A need for dominance: Power-driven people or people who like to feel in charge or be in charge need to keep their status safe. So, they find a way always to be the one in charge and take control of situations. They have to manipulate people and exhibit dominance over them. Some people tend to feel a sense of satisfaction and superiority from feeling above others, and to achieve this, they manipulate people into being their pawns sometimes unconsciously and sometimes consciously on the part of the manipulator and the person being manipulated.

Lack of social skills to handle certain issues: Some people's inability to handle issues properly or expertly makes them seek succor in manipulating others in a bid to cover up for their poor social skills or inadequacies. Since they can't find something else to resort to, they stick to manipulation, always using it as a cover-up and hideout. Some manipulative techniques they make use of are lying, evasion, diversion, feigning confusion, or innocence.

Truth Detection: Detectives are one of the professionals that make proper use of Psychological Manipulation in this century. They use this technique to extract the undiluted truth from the criminals even when they are not ready to confess. My doubt for this truth-detection psychological manipulation fades away any time I remember how my friend's dad, many years back, used it to get my stubborn friend without any struggle.

It happened that my friend had stolen an amount of money from his dad the previous day but would never confess if anyone asked. His dad's silence made him think he [his dad] didn't notice the missing money, not knowing that the manipulative father was waiting for the perfect moment to throw his manipulation skill at him. I went to visit him that afternoon when his dad called me in his presence and began like: "You know what? When you're smart, you're smart. Nothing can take that from you. And I'm glad I gave birth to a smart boy." He said, smiling and pointing to my friend who brought his attention to what his father was telling me. The father continued;

"In this house as a whole, I am the best person that knows how to keep things, especially money, which means it will take an extremely smart child to discover where I keep my money. I was wowed yesterday by my son's smartness to discover where that money was kept, and I just had to applaud him." He paused again, clapping and smiling. I was smiling too while looking at my friend and saying in my mind, "wow! John must be very smart truly," not knowing that a manipulation game was being played on us. John too was already smiling in agreement to what his dad was saying then the father slotted in the targeted question;

"So, John, have you spent everything or it's remaining little? Please quickly give me $90 out of it, I want to attend to something urgently." He said he didn't care about the money. John fell for the trick, and diligently went into his room to bring out the stolen money without uttering a word.

"Wow! So, you're the one who stole my money! I will deal with you today!" The dad's reaction changed, and that was when I realized that it wasn't all real from the beginning. John could have denied it if confronted without manipulation, but he couldn't say anything except the truth when being trapped with the power of manipulation.

Motives Compared; Then and Now

The motives that drove manipulation in the past have evolved, and objectives have gradually changed as the art is now close to inevitability nowadays. Then, manipulation was used during warfare to have the upper hand over the opponents or gain victory over the enemy, government propagandist also used manipulation, and then there were little bits of manipulation in interpersonal relationships. Manipulation was then largely considered as devilish, deceitful, and something only the powerful could do.

However, as the years rolled by, and situations began to change, the world started to evolve, and the art of manipulation also had its fair share in the evolution process. Manipulation left the stage of being a tool for powerful and tyrannical individuals; Government, police, warriors, leaders, to be a tool for smart and goal-oriented individuals; Professionals.

The motives behind manipulation than were directed towards ultimately obtaining power or exhibiting power, showcasing strength, skills, and manipulative capacity, threatening and oppressing or punishing. Government and leaders also used manipulation to control the masses through propaganda where they played and preyed simultaneously on the masses' minds while they

Manipulation then, to an extent, exerted the use of force, even though in the present age, physical manipulation still exists; back in the days, it was more in use. It was used in policing activities to get culprits to confess their crimes, it was used by leaders to punish offenders and by tyrannical rulers to exhibit power. Physical manipulation was also used in battles and wars where enemies confronted each other and played on each other's mind while also taking advantage of the opponent's bodily strength or weakness.

These days, however, the narrative seems to have changed as the art of manipulation is now used even more unconsciously than ever before. The extent to which media manipulation has permeated the air and has unconsciously gotten people with their effective and persuasive messages is evidence of how the manipulation tale has evolved. You can now manipulate people through the media and get them to act in certain ways without even coming in contact with them.

Manipulation is now used for more purposeful, positive and impactful reasons by getting people to act certain ways to get desirable effects all for the good of the individual as well as the good of the manipulator or society. It is no longer that one-sided art that is in the sole interest of the manipulator; it is now a titfor-tat mechanism. People in business that positively manipulate clients do so with an interest of the client also in mind, counsellors or therapists manipulate patients for their good, so the manipulation chain while being for the interest of the manipulator is also somewhat rewarding for the person being manipulated. But then again, whatever act of manipulation that is done is solely determined by the intent of the manipulator, either it's positive or negative. The change between the motives of manipulation then and manipulation now is the fact that it has now taken a subtler and smarter approach compared to how it was back in the days. Even though motives such as ego, quest for power, lack of social skills, fear still share a common relationship between motives then and motives now.

Chapter 7 Covert Emotional Manipulation/ Methods

Covert emotional manipulation is used by people who want to gain power or control over you by deploying tactics that are both deceptive and underhanded. Such people want to change the way you think and behave without you ever realizing what it is they are doing. In other words, they use techniques that can alter your perceptions in such a way that you think that you are doing it out of your own free will. Covert emotional manipulation is "covert" because it works without you being consciously aware of that fact. People who are good at deploying such techniques can get you to do their bidding without your knowledge; they can hold you "psychologically captive." When skilled manipulators set their sights on you, they can get you to grant them power over your emotional well-being and even your self-worth. They will put you under their spell without you even realizing it. They will win your trust, and you will start attaching value to what they think of you. Once you have let them into your life, they will then start chipping away at your very identity in a methodical way, and as time goes by, you will lose your self-esteem and turn into whatever they want you to be.

Covert emotional manipulation is more common than you might think. Since it's subtle, people are rarely aware that it's happening to them, and in some cases, they may never even notice. Only keen outside observers may be able to tell when this form of manipulation is going on.

You might know someone who used to be fun and jovial, then she got into a relationship with someone else, and a few years down the line, she seems to have a completely different personality. If it's an old friend, you might not even recognize the person she has become. That is how powerful covert emotional manipulation can be. It can completely overhaul someone's personality without them even realizing it. The manipulator will chip away at you little by little, and you will accept minute changes that fly under the radar, until the old you are replaced by a different version of you, build to be subservient to the manipulator.

Covert emotional manipulation works like a slow-moving coup. It requires you to make small progressive concessions to the person that is trying to manipulate you. In other words, you let go of tiny aspects of your identity to accommodate the manipulative person, so it never registers in your mind that there is something bigger at play.

When the manipulative person pushes you to change in small ways, you will comply because you don't want to "sweat the small stuff." However, there is a domino effect that occurs as you start conceding to the manipulative person. You will be more comfortable making subsequent concessions, and your personality will be erased and replaced in a cumulative progression.

Covert emotional manipulation occurs to some extent in all social dynamics. Let's look at how it plays out in romantic relationships, in friendships, and at work.

Emotional Manipulation In Relationships

There is a lot of emotional manipulation that takes place in romantic relationships, and it's not always malicious. For example, women try to modify men's behavior to make them more "housebroken"; that is just normal. However, there are certain instances of manipulation where the person's intention is malicious, and he/she is motivated by a need to control or dominate over the other person.

Positive reinforcement is perhaps the most used covert manipulation technique in romantic relationships. Your partner can get you to do what he wants by praising you, flattering you, giving you attention, offering your gifts, and acting affectionately.

Even the seemingly nice things in relationships can turn out to be covert manipulation tools and props. For instance, your girlfriend could use intense sex as a weapon to reinforce a certain kind of behavior in you. Similarly, men can use charm, appreciation, or gifts to reinforce certain behaviors in the women they are dating.

Some sophisticated manipulators use what psychologists call "intermittent positive reinforcement" to gain control over their partners. The way it works is that the perpetrator will shower the victim with intense positive reinforcement for a certain period of time, then switch to just giving her normal levels of attention and appreciation. After a random interval of time, he will again go back to the intense positive reinforcement. When the victim gets used to the special treatment, it's taken away, and when she gets used to normal treatment, the special treatment is brought back, and it all seems arbitrary. Now, the victim will get to a place where she becomes sort of "addicted" to the special treatment, but she has no idea how to get it, so she starts doing whatever the perpetrator wants in the hope that one of the things she does will bring back the intense positive reinforcement. In other words, she effectively becomes subservient to the perpetrator.

Negative reinforcement techniques are also used in relationships to manipulate others covertly. For example, partners can withhold sex as a way of compelling the other person to modify their behavior in a specific way. People also use techniques such as the silent treatment, and withholding of love and affection.

Some malicious people can create a false sense of intimacy by pretending to open up to you. They could share personal stories and talk about their hopes and fears. When they do this, they create the impression that they trust you, but their intention may be to get you to feel a sense of obligation towards them. Manipulators also use well-calculated insinuations to get you to react in a certain way at the moment to modify your behavior in the long run. Such insinuations can be made through words or even actions. In colloquial terms, we call this "dropping a hint." People in relationships are always trying to figure out what the other person wants out of that relationship, so a manipulative person can drop hints to get you to do what they want without ever having to take responsibility for the actions that you take because they can always argue that you misinterpreted what they meant.

However, malicious insinuations can be very hurtful, and they can chip away at your self-esteem. Your partner can insinuations to suggest you are gaining weight, you aren't making enough money, or even to suggest that your cooking skills aren't any good. People use insinuations to get away with "saying without saying," any number of hurtful things that could affect your selfesteem.

Emotional Manipulations In Friendships

Covert emotional manipulation is quite common in friendships and casual relationships. Friendships tend to progress slower than romantic relationships, but that just means that it can take a lot more time for you to figure out if your friends are manipulative. Manipulation in friendships can be confusing because even well-meaning friends can come across as malicious. That's because there is a certain social rivalry that exists between even the closest of friends, which explains the concept of "frenemies."

Manipulative friends tend to be passive-aggressive. This is where they manipulate you into doing what they want by involving mutual friends rather than by coming to you directly. Passive aggression works as a manipulation technique because it denies you a chance of directly addressing whatever issue your friend is raising, and so in a manner of speaking, you lose by default.

For example, if a friend wants you to do her a favor, instead of coming out and asking you, she goes to a mutual friend and suggests that she asks you on her behalf. Now, when the mutual friend approaches you, it becomes very difficult for you to turn down the request because there is added social pressure. When you say no, your whole social circle now perceives you as selfish. Passive aggression can also involve the use of silent treatment to get you to comply with a request. Imagine a situation where one of your friends talks to everyone else but you. It's going to be incredibly awkward for you, and everyone will start prying, wondering what the issue is between the two of you, and taking sides on the matter.

Friends can also covertly manipulate you by using subtle insults. They can give you back-handed compliments that have hidden meanings. When you take the time to think about what they meant by the compliment, you will realize that it's an insult in disguise, and that will bruise your self-esteem, and possibly modify your behavior.

Some friends can manipulate you by going on a "power trip" and trying to control your social interactions. For example, there are those friends who are going to insist that every time you hang out, it should be in their apartment, or at a social venue of their choosing. Such friends often have the intention of dominating your friendship, so they are keen to always have the "home ground advantage" over you. They'll try to push you out of your comfort zone, just so that you can reveal your weaknesses and you can then become more emotionally reliant on them.   Manipulative friends tend to excessively capitalize on your friendship, and to a disproportionate degree. They will ask you for lots of favors with no regard for your time or your effort. They are the kinds of friends who will leverage your friendship every time they need something, but then make excuses when it's their turn to reciprocate.

Emotional Manipulation At Work

There are many reasons why your colleague may want to manipulate you. It could be you are on the same career path, and so he wants to make you look bad. It could be that he is lazy, and he wants to stick you with his responsibilities. It could also be that he is a sadist, and he just wants to see you suffer. One-way people at work exert their dominance over others is by stressing them out and then, almost immediately, relieving the stress. Say, for example, you make a minor error on a report, and your boss calls you into his office. He makes a big fuss and threatens to fire you, but then towards the end, he switches gears and reassures you that your job is secure as long as you do what he wants. That kind of manipulation works on people because it makes them afraid and gives them a sense of obligation at the same time.

Some colleagues can manipulate you by doing you small favors, and then reminding you of those favors every time they want something from you. For instance, if you made an error at work and a colleague covered for you, he may hold it over your head for months or even years to come, and he is going to guilt you into feeling indebted to him.

Colleagues can also manipulate you by leaving you out of the loop when they are passing across important information. The intention here is to get you to mess up so that they can have a better standing with the boss or with other colleagues. When you discover that someone is leaving you out of the loop at work and you confront them, they could feign innocence and pretend that it was a genuine mistake on their part, or they could find a way to turn it around and blame you.

People with dark personality traits tend to be hyper-competitive at work, and they won't hesitate to use underhanded means to pull one over you. Most colleagues turn out to be good friends, but you should be careful with colleagues that are overly eager to befriend you. It could be that they want to learn more about you so that they can figure out your strengths and weaknesses and find ways to use them against you. Narcissists, Machiavellians, and psychopaths are very good at scheming at work, so don't let them catch you off guard.

Chapter 8 Mind Control With NLP For Love And Relationship

Mind control techniques are extremely powerful because they don't just change how a person feels or acts; they fundamentally change that person's entire belief system. That is why, of all the manipulation and influence techniques out there, NLP's mind control is by far the most dangerous.

Most people find the concept of NLP's mind control fascinating. That's because, as humans, we are reluctant to believe that someone else could take charge of the way we process thoughts and emotions, and use us like puppets to his advantage. We all like to think that we are intelligent, mentally strong, and we will be able to see any attempts at mind control coming from a mile away and to shut it down immediately.

That is a misconception that we need to dispel. Mind control can happen to the best of us. With concerted effort, even the brightest people can abandon their beliefs and their curated thinking patterns and take on new ones. In most cases, mind control happens slowly and progressively, and the consequences are realized long before the victim is aware of whatever is going on.

Your mind takes in a lot of information at any given time, and it only processes a small fraction of that information. If you are looking straight ahead of you, just within your life of sight, there are thousands of details that you fail to notice, and your brain only pays attention to the details that it thinks are important. Sight is just one of the five senses you have. At any given time, you are taking in information through each of those senses without being consciously aware of that fact.

So, both your conscious and unconscious mind filters out information so that you are only aware of the "important" details. The filtration process depends on the prevailing conditions in the brain. That explains why two people who are perceiving the same exact thing often come up with different interpretations of what's going on.

NLP's mind control techniques work through a concept known as "priming." You can prime someone to think certain pieces of information are more important than others so that when they encounter certain sensory stimuli, the specific details pass through the filters. They register in the person's mind. Let's look at an example that explains how the brain filters information and how priming can work: a man gets home in the evening, and his wife tells him that she is pregnant. They celebrate, and he goes to sleep with the thought of having a baby at the back of his mind. The next day when he goes to work, he starts noticing baby-related things that he has never noticed before; he sees "baby on board" stickers on every other car as he drives to work, notices lots of people pushing babies in strollers around the neighborhood, he spots a daycare center somewhere along the road. When he gets to the office, he notices that some of his colleagues have pictures of their infant children on their desks.

The man in the example above has always seen those "babyrelated" things every day, but they never register in his mind, because at the time, he didn't consider those details to be necessary. Now that his impending fatherhood is at the back of his mind, everything that suggests the word "baby" passes through all of his filters. His brain is unconsciously processing this information, so it grasps upon anything that contributes to his body of knowledge about the subject.

In this case, you can say that the man has been "primed" to think about babies.

NLP mind control makes use of priming techniques that are more subtle than the one we have discussed above, but it works the same way. Someone can prime you to consider specific ideas and sensory stimuli as necessary; that way, they will be able to guide your thought process and ultimately control the way you feel about certain things, or the way you act in response to certain stimuli.

Your actions are the result of your thoughts, your feelings, and your assumptions (assumptions are generally based on past experiences). NLP techniques comprise of meticulously designed strategies that may introduce certain stimuli to the mind in a predetermined pattern so that the person can act predictably.

Understanding Conscious and Subconscious Perception

Your perceptions are influenced by the stimuli in your surroundings, whether or not you are consciously aware of the presence of those stimuli. If someone introduces a stimulus in your vicinity, it can bypass your conscious mind and end up in your subconscious mind. The conscious mind has a way of ignoring "mundane" details and only noticing things that have to be regarded with urgency.

Even though the information that bypasses your conscious won't be treated with urgency, your brain will still think of it as important or significant, and it may act upon it at a later time when a related stimulus is introduced to your mind. Here is a classic mental trick that can be used to demonstrate how this concept works:

A handful of people go into a meeting, and the person who was officiating that meeting is wearing a red tie. The tie is certainly noticeable (it's a bright color, so it stands out), but no one thinks about it consciously. They focus on what efficiency is saying. Throughout the meeting, he keeps dropping the word "read" into his speech (these words sound vaguely similar to the word "red"). At the end of the meeting, he mentions that a follow-up meeting would be held early the next day.

When the next day comes around and the previous attendees show up to the follow-up meeting, most of them are wearing at least one red-colored item of clothing.

In this example, he uses related stimuli (the red tie and the word "read") to induce a certain specific though in his colleagues' minds. His trick works because his suggestions are very subtle. If he had gone ahead and used the word "red" in his speech, his colleagues would have made a conscious connection between the colors of his time and the word, and then they wouldn't be subconsciously primed to wear the color red the next day. So, NLP only works if the suggestions fly under the radar.

Now Let's Look at NLP Mind Control Techniques

If you want to use NLP to control someone's mind, the first thing you need to do is pay close attention to them. You have to study them for a while so that you can understand their cues, including their eye movements, their breathing patterns, their eye dilation patterns, the way their faces become flushed in response to certain stimuli, their nervous tics, etc.

Studying your target helps you understand their emotional state as well as their baseline behavior. Those observations can indicate to you how a person takes in and processes information. For example, if you pay attention to a person's eye movements, you can conclude that he processes information through visual creativity if he looks up and to the right before responding to questions about colors of specific objects. You can conclude that he processes information through visual recollection if his eyes move up and to the left.

Even if you don't fully understand the technical interpretations of the person's cues, you can still use them as a roadmap to track any changes as you attempt to control their minds.

When using NLP to implant ideas into a person's mind, it's more effective if you speak with a "suggestive frequency." This is the frequency that matches the rate at which the human heartbeats. Under normal circumstances, the human heartbeats as the rate of 45 to 72 beats per minute, so you can put your target's mind in a highly suggestible state if you speak at about 60 words a minute (give or take ten words). This trick is often used in hypnosis.

To bypass your target's conscious mind, you can use the "voice roll" technique. This is where you deliver your words in a specific pattern and pace with the aim of stressing certain points without raising the alarm in the conscious mind. You can emphasize the words that you want to entrench in the person's subconscious, but you have to use a monotonous tone to avoid making them notice what you are doing.

As you subconsciously program your target, you have to introduce an "anchor." An anchor is a specific stimulus that can return someone to a particular conscious state if it were to be reintroduced later on. For example, you can tap someone on the shoulder when he is in a particular state of mind. The stimulus (the feeling of being touched on the shoulder) will be linked to that particular state. So, when the person's conscious state starts to change, you always have the option of touching them on the shoulder again and drawing them back to the desired state. You can also control someone's mind by covertly establishing a rapport with them. This can be done by mirroring your target's body language in a positive way so that they feel connected to you, and comfortable enough to be receptive to your other NLP techniques.

As you deploy your NLP mind control strategy, you can make use of "hot words" to make your words more effective. Hot words are common words that can create strong connections to certain senses in a person. For example, words such as now, see, feel free, because, hear, etc. have a way of invoking certain senses or mental states.

Now, let's look at how a typical NLP mind control strategy would play out if all the techniques are used in conjunction with each other.

First, you identify your target and start studying him or her. Here, you want to figure out which side of his brain is the dominant one (you can use the person's handedness as a guide in this case; in most cases, right-handed people have a dominant left hemisphere, and left-handed people have a dominant right hemisphere). You also want to know what their dominant sense is (most people have all their five senses, but in every person, one sense often seems to be more dominant than the others). You also want to know how their brain stores and accesses information (you can figure this out by observing the person's eye movements as we discussed earlier in this chapter). You also want to be able to tell how they behave when they are lying or when they are making up information instead of recalling it.

Secondly, you have to establish a rapport with the person (you can use the mirroring technique we discussed earlier). Once the rapport has been established, you now have to keep interacting with the person as you subtly steer them in the direction you want. You can use the voice techniques and the language patterns we've mentioned.

When you are looking to steer someone in a certain direction, you can use anchoring and elicitation. We have already discussed anchoring, but it's important to mention that when you are selecting an anchor, you should choose one that is unique, one that you can control on cue. If you use an anchor that is commonplace (such as coughing, nodding your head, etc.), you could accidentally trigger it at an inconvenient moment, and that will ruin your NLP strategies.

Elicitation involves the use of subtle nudges or suggestions to bet someone to reveal certain things about themselves. Here, you have to prime your target to volunteer certain information about himself without realizing what is happening. You can then use that information to manipulate the person further. Remember that when you use NLP, your aim is to engineer certain responses, not to get the person to act completely out of character. It's about introducing subtle suggestions that nudge the person in a specific direction, not overhauling who they are. So, NLP can help a salesman sell a product to a reluctant customer, or it can help a grafter swindle money from a mark, but as a standalone technique, it cannot be used to convince someone to join a cult or to commit murder.

You can use NLP mind control to condition yourself to deal with certain situations. For example, you can introduce an anchor on yourself when you are in a positive emotional state (i.e., when you are happy, motivated, and productive). When you find yourself slipping into a negative emotional state (egg if you as sad or stressed), you can trigger your anchor, and then you'd find yourself going back to your positive state.

NLP mind control can benefit you if you use it on yourself to improve your mental state, or if you use it on others to get what you want from them, but what happens if a malicious person uses these techniques on you?

You need to learn to guard against NLP's mind control. The following tips can help you identify and prevent NLP mind control:

First, you should be highly cautious when you realize that someone is copying your body language. Mirroring happens naturally, and it can be a sign that someone likes you or feels comfortable around you, but if you are dealing with a stranger (or a person you know who might be into NLP), you should put your shield up once you sense something is up.

When someone seems to be holding eye contact with you and tracking your eye movements, they could be attempting to figure out your baseline brain activity, and how you store and access information, so try moving your eyes in random patterns.

At the very least, this will confuse them, and they won't be able to calibrate you properly.

If a person is acting suspiciously, don't let him touch you. He may be introducing an anchor in your subconscious to prime you to react in a specific way. If you experience certain heightened emotions and a person touches you (say on the shoulder), make it clear to them that they are not allowed to touch you again (so they won't be able to use the anchor they have just created).

Watch out for language that seems overly permissive. For example, if a person keeps saying things like "feel free to relax," they could be attempting to put you in a relaxed mental state. On the same point, you should also watch out for language that seems unnecessarily vague. When you listen to vague ideas, you are more likely to slip into a hypnotic trance, and this opens the door for a manipulator to control your mind. The same goes for language that sounds like gibberish. When you hear gibberish for a prolonged period of time, your conscious mind will start to switch off, but your subconscious will be fully awake, and it will be receptive to whatever the person is saying.

You should also pay attention to the subtext of what the person is saying to avoid NLP mind control. NLP experts can program you by saying seemingly normal things, but their words may be played with hidden meanings. Earlier in the chapter, we looked at an example where a person uses the word "read" to imply

the color "red." NLP experts can build such layers into the words they choose to use, and they may influence you without your knowledge.

Chapter 9 Using NLP To Avoid Manipulation

Neuro-Linguistic Programming is defined as a set of skills that reveal the kind of communication that matters most – on the inside and out. Neuro refers to the brain/mind and, more so, how it affects behaviors and communication. Linguistic refers to the ways we reveal the state of our mind and body through verbal and nonverbal communication. Programming refers to the potential of changing the state of our body and mind. A person who knows NLP can understand his or her mind and the minds of other people and the conversations going on within. Such a person will understand how the mind of a person works under certain circumstances. Consequently, he/she can change the way the person thinks gradually. Does that mean that a manipulator can change the use of NLP to control his/her victims?

Manipulation is defined as attempting to influence or influencing the behaviors or emotions of others for one's purpose. However, manipulation does not have to have a negative outcome for the victim. Neuro-linguistic programming can be manipulative in this way too. Simply put, the outcome of NLP will depend on the practitioner using it and his/her intentions. A marketer or salesperson may use these techniques to persuade a customer to purchase products. Another person may use the skills to extort money from the other. It can be used to get you to agree with things you would ordinarily disagree with.

Most people using NLP want to manipulate a person into feeling better and being more resourceful. They help a person to set goals, solve problems, identify exactly what is going on in their lives, fix a mental condition such as phobia, or inspire them to be great. However, there are those people who will use NPL for selfish purposes. It is okay to deal with NLP practitioners who have good intentions, such as therapists, motivational speakers, among others. But you need to be wary of the people trying to manipulate you negatively using the Neuro-linguistic programming techniques. What should you look out for?   First, watch out for people copying your body language. If you notice that a person talking to you is copying the way you sit or fold your hands, do a test by changing your style or making new movements. If the other person does the same, you have a manipulator at hand. A manipulator who is skilled at using NLP will not have a hard time making these changes, but a new one will immediately follow you. It is a good time to question the person.

Secondly, move your eyes randomly. A person seeking to manipulate you will closely listen to your words and eye movement. When a person is watching your eyes and face closely while having a conversation, you might think that he/she is interested in your story. That is hardly the case. A manipulator will be observing the way you store and access information. The movements of your eyes can give you away. A good manipulator using NLP will be able to tell what you are thinking in a few hours. He/she will be able to tell when you are lying or telling the truth. Consequently, they will be able to predict your next move and use it to their advantage. A safer way of avoiding this kind of manipulation is to move your eyes randomly. Look around, and right left up down in predictable patterns. Ensure that the movements seem natural. This will drive the manipulator crazy as he/she is unable to read you. Thirdly do not allow a person to touch you. As crazy as it sounds, something as simple as a tap on your shoulder can alter your emotions. A manipulator who is knowledgeable in NLP will know when you pay your back or tap your shoulder to anchor you. In simpler terms, you might be having a conversation with a person, and you are laughing, then the person taps your shoulder. This is called anchoring, and it gives the person the power to put you back in that state later by touching you in the same place. Do not allow a potential manipulator to touch you. Fourthly, look out for vague language. One of the NLP techniques recommended by Milton Erickson involves the use of vague language. It has been found that vague language can be used to lead people into a trance. On the other hand, specific languages keep people alert, thus hard to manipulate. If a person is using a language so simple that you do not need to think hard, look closer. You might be manipulated.

Fifthly, look out for permissive language. If a person makes a statement like "Feel free to relax," be very wary. Such permissive language takes a person into a trance. A manipulator will make you feel comfortable before striking. According to NLP, the easiest way of allowing someone to make you do something is by letting them permit you.

Again, look out for gibberish. If a person says something like "As we move towards the center of the mater, you will find yourself in line with the look of success than in the previous times" that sentence is so complicated, yet the message can be passed more straightforwardly. In such a case, tell the person to be more specific. "Can you please elaborate?" "Please tell exactly what that means." Manipulators are very good at using words to confuse you. They are never direct with their intention. If you feel that something is not clear, ask for an explanation. It is also important to Read between the lines. Many people are not direct with their intentions, especially when they want to manipulate others. Be on the lookout for hidden messages. A master manipulator will hide their intentions in statements. They will also avoid giving you time to think. You will find that your time for replying is very limited. Also, their questions predetermine your answer. For instance, "That place is very beautiful; don't you agree we should visit it?" Do not subconsciously agree with what others say. Take your time to understand the question.

Do not agree with a manipulator. If a person is making you agree with them quickly, it is better to say no. Do not rush into decisions influenced by emotions. TAKE your time and let the person know that you need to consider a few things before giving an answer. Use a rational mind to analyze the statements.

Finally, trust your instincts. If your intuition shows you that a person is playing with you, it is probably right. This is one of the main rules you should apply in life. It is important to walk away from such a situation or engage in a defensive way. However, it is advisable to avoid engaging manipulators; they might find a way to convince you.

Chapter 10 What Is The Dark Psychology?

Dark psychology refers to the ability to manipulate and control the minds of others. It typically entails both manipulation and coercion. In the wrong hands, it can be devastating, but understanding what it is can be the difference between being manipulated as a target yourself and being able to use the concepts within dark psychology without falling victim to the darkness at its core. You can use the ideas without being evil or malicious, though there is quite a fine line between using it ethically and falling into the darkness.

What Is Dark Psychology?

At its root, dark psychology is all about mind control. You can influence what other people think or do by understanding the inner workings of the other person's mind. You can persuade them into behaving in certain ways, making them feel as though what they have done is of their own volition even though you were behind the scenes, orchestrating the actions the entire time. You can motivate people to help you by helping them first. You know that they are more likely to offer help if you help them first simply because people tend to reciprocate. When you understand how the minds of those around you work, you can begin utilizing it to your advantage

Uses Of Dark Psychology

Dark psychology is used widely throughout a wide range of scenarios, some of which are more sinister, while others are typically seen as far less harmful. Each of the following groups utilizes concepts included in dark psychology to get desired results: Religion, politics, cults, terrorist organizations, abusers, and salespeople all rely heavily on the concepts of dark psychology, pulling strings behind the backs of other people to get what they want.

Religion

Religion is all about conformity. You are expected to conform to a certain set of beliefs, into which you most frequently indoctrinated as children and then encouraged to follow through adulthood. Religion, though it may seem harmless, actually uses several dark psychology techniques to keep people in line and to follow the doctrine. Typically, this is seen as some sort of threat or punishment if you do not follow through — it could be going to hell instead of some sort of paradise or heaven after death, or it could be a threat of ex-communication and abandonment. These threats play upon two huge fears of people — losing community and a threat of eternal suffering, and people are more likely to obey.

Politics

Political leaders often engage in several different dark psychology techniques that are useful in manipulating the minds of other people. They hold themselves certain ways, word things in ways that make the people believe they can better empathize, and speaking in ways that inspire other people to follow them. They often use slippery slope fear-mongering tactics, promising results that no one will like if people oppose them. They use stances meant to convey power and authority, and people fall for it. People fall for the artificial body language that the politicians use, and the politicians win out.

Cults

Cults, especially destructive cults, are incredibly exploitative. They are considered totalistic — meaning they seek to gain control over the other person entirely. They frequently engage in various forms of thought reform to gain control over the other person's mind. These cults rely on authoritarian following and leading into a wide range of manipulative tactics. Cults rely on their leaders' charisma, deception, isolation, methods of thought-reform, demands for loyalty and devotion, creating a divide between those who follow the cult and outsiders, cult language or jargon that is difficult to understand and follow if you are not a member and as much control as possible over the day-to-day existence of the members. All of this culminates in a group that seeks to manipulate and control the members in a way that demands absolute loyalty. This is how people get sucked in — they are drawn in with false promises, and their personality and thoughts are whittled away, bit by bit, day by day until finally, all that is left behind is a tool for the cult to use. When under the control of the cult's leaders, the leader can command nearly anything, and the followers will do so. This is what makes them so destructive — the members are essentially turned into mindless weapons, willing to do whatever it takes to stay in favor.

Terrorism

Terrorism groups follow similar methods as cults to get people in line — promising the world for their absolute devotion. They draw people in with idealized values and charismatic leaders and whittle the people away until they are willing to do anything, even if it involves suicide. They see themselves as a part of the whole, a part of the change that they will use to change the world for the better, and they are glad to give their very lives, or the lives of their loved ones, to achieve it.

Abuse

Abusers love to utilize dark psychology — they use the inner workings of the minds to weasel their ways into the lives of their victims and firmly root themselves as integral members while taking advantage of people's tendencies to want to keep their relationships meaningful. The abuser love bombs the victim, meaning he showers the victim in love, attention, and affection to hook the victim to him before suddenly revoking the attention, making the victim crave it and do anything necessary to get the love back. This sort of manipulation tactic and use of dark psychology is often seen with narcissists, in particular, to understand what the narcissist wants.

Sales

Even something as innocent as sales can be littered with dark psychology tactics. The best salespeople can intuitively convince people to buy, tapping into unconscious tendencies, appeals to emotions, and even hijacking the other person's body language to achieve the desired result. Salespeople get paid based on their sales, so they will do anything necessary to get the desired results. They will appeal to a parent's fear of a car accident to upsell to a safer vehicle. They will use a person's near-death experience as a segue into selling life insurance. They will change their body language to convince the other person, picking up on small cues here and there and acting upon them to get the desired results.

Identifying Dark Psychology

Often, identifying whether you are being manipulated is difficult. The entire purpose of many of these manipulation or coercion tactics is that they are unnoticeable. They happen so seamlessly that the individual being manipulated never realizes it is happening. You wait until they are fully hooked before yanking the line and getting the results you want, and because of this patient, end-game type of behavior, the one being manipulated never realizes it.

However, there are frequently subtle signs that manipulation or coercion is happening. These signs tend to be overlooked by people that feel as though they are overthinking, especially if the manipulator is someone trusted and ensures that they are thinking about things too much. Often these red flags involve the victim's behaviors and feelings.

One of the biggest identifiers is intuition — you may feel as though something is wrong, but you go along with it anyway. Often, this happens with people who are less self-confident and are more willing to push off their thoughts. These people tend to be targeted individuals simply because they are easy to manipulate — they do the hard part themselves! They convince themselves not to worry or that what is going on is not a big deal, and that allows for the manipulator to get their way easier. Another huge red flag is when you catch yourself thinking something that you never thought would be your thoughts. You likely have been influenced by someone else to take that position, even though it is not one that you naturally would lean toward. When this happens, especially if your thought is one that causes that feeling of cognitive dissonance triggered at the conflict between thought and belief, you may want to reevaluate whether things are going according to plan.

One more red flag is feeling isolated and pressured in some way. People with honest intentions will not lay down the pressure to make decisions immediately when it is not a life-or-death situation. You can wait the day to decide on whether to buy the car or house. You should be able to speak it over with your spouse, friends, or family to bounce ideas back and forth. If you feel as though those close to you are being cut out of your life for some reason in some way, there is probably a reason for that feeling, and it is that you are being manipulated.

Resisting Dark Psychology

To resist dark psychology, you must first be aware of some of the ways people become susceptible to it in the first place. Most frequently, these people are those who are trusting and empathetic. They are willing to take the word of someone else on how something is going because they do not feel as though people in this world are manipulative. However, people are manipulative. People can be evil. People will use others, especially if they will benefit. Those who use dark psychology for malicious reasons tend to have no qualms about sacrificing others, so long as they get their desired results.

Those with lower self-esteem also tend to be easy targets. They will trust the words of the manipulator at face value, making them easily convinced that they are wrong, or that they have interpreted things incorrectly. They will even convince themselves of that if they are given a chance.

With that in mind, there are three easy tips for avoiding or resisting dark psychology.

Trust your gut

You should always, at the very least, listen to your gut reactions. While these can be unreliable and can be swayed sometimes, you can also use them to notice when something seems wrong. If you feel as though something is wrong, or you get that pit in your stomach that signals you are uncomfortable in some way, shape, or form, you should listen to it. Take that as a cue to be vigilant and do not try to quash the feeling. You should not try to discredit your intuition — it serves a valuable purpose. You should stop and analyze your situation, determining whether or not the gut feeling is correct. Once you trust that gut feeling, you can move on to step two: Fact-checking.

Question and fact check

Never be afraid to ask questions, especially if you get that nagging feeling in your gut. You should ask questions, challenge the other person, and be willing to ask for evidence or doublecheck what has been said. For example, if you are shopping for a used car, feel free to ask as many questions as you want. Push the point, ask for reports on the vehicle. If the other person seems to resist, they may be being dishonest or deceptive somehow. If you hear something in a presidential candidate debate or during a political speech, you should fact-check everything before accepting it as true. People will skew how they present things to get the desired results, and you should always be aware of that. If someone is attempting to pressure you, do not feel as though you must give in and instead ask yourself why you should. Question if the behavior is correct if it matches up with your ideas, and how it is beneficial. If you can stop and see behaviors or attempts to manipulate for what they are, you are not going to be nearly as susceptible. If your spouse bothers you to do something, but you feel uncomfortable with it, it is okay to question why you should do something and make the decision of your own volition rather than merely giving in to the other person's appeal to authority.

Build self-esteem

Since the most susceptible to manipulation and coercion are those who suffer from low self-esteem, building that self-esteem up is crucial. Doing so means that you will not try to downplay your reactions to it. By building self-confidence, you essentially tell yourself that you are a reliable judge of what is happening around you and what should continue to happen around you. You can determine whether things are right or wrong, and you recognize that your positions on matters are accurate. By deciding this, you can resist attempts to browbeat you into believing the other person's narration. You will trust your narration enough not to be swayed.

Chapter 11 The Dark Triad: Narcissism, Machiavellianism, Psychopathy

Within each of us, we all have both a light and dark side. The extent of exhibiting the light vs. dark motif of feelings, thoughts, and behaviors vary from one and other.

The umbrella of " dark triads" subsumes various personality traits that are linked to mainly three classes of behavior. These classes are Machiavellianism, Narcissism, and Psychopathy. These behaviors are ethically, socially, and morally questionable but still are part of everyday life.

The illustrations of exploitative, selfish, ruthless, and incredibly evil behaviors are part of history and cultures across the world. With time supposedly distinct dark triads are increasing severely. These increasingly narrow dark traits are resulting in a superfluity of erect lacking theoretical consolidations. But do we understand what dark triad is?

What Is Dark Triad?

Do you have any concept of the Bermuda triangle??

The dark triad is just like the Bermuda triangle. Narcissism, Machiavellianism, and psychopathy are its three corners. It is dangerous to get near it. Similar to the Bermuda triangle, it is all three traits that often overlap and introduce a damaging, toxic, and brutal personality.

This term was introduced in 2002 by Paulus and Williams. The dark triad is the combination of three unusual and negative psyche triads. Two of these personality triads share more similar characters other than with Narcissism.

The dark triad refers to an individual having some "subclinical" symptoms. Most probably, the dark triad has collective features of antisocial personality disorder (ASPD) and narcissist personality disorder (NPD). Machiavellianism is not a mental disorder. This concept of the dark triad is also termed as Dfactor. According to the latest research presence of one dark personality, triad increases the probability of having another dark trait also.

Modern studies have revealed the nine dark personality triads, but a person with some of these D-factors doesn't need to have an antisocial personality disorder.

To understand DARK TRIAD, it is essential to get the concept of three major classes of behaviors:

Machiavellianism

Machiavellianism is a dark triad that is more common in men, but it can, however, appear in anyone, even in children also.

This term is reference derived from a philosopher and a diplomat Niccolo M Machiavelli.

"According to the psychological explanation of Machiavellianism is a personality trait that refers to the unemotional people who manipulate and regularly deceive others."

They never think about the emotions, feelings, and loss of others and remain bounded in their world of interests. The person with Machiavellianism believes in:

· Flattering wise people for their interest.

· Never tell the root cause behind any action unless they feel it useful to do so.

· They always remain busy in getting corners here and there to get ahead.

· They assume it safe to be heartless or vicious.

Signs Of Machiavellianism:

In today's world, you can observe most of the people carrying the torch of Machiavellianism. Even you can also be a Machiavellian yourself, but you wouldn't even aware of this fact. The ideology of Machiavellianism is based upon ambiguous cunning, fraudulent, controlling, and manipulation. It is the selfish conduction of selves to acquire other people to do what you want them to do.

Machiavellians do anything to get what they desire for even they walk over the people if it is in need. They are very much focused on their interests and never think about the hazards and troubles they can create for others.

The person with Machiavellianism possesses the following traits.

Signs of duplicity:

Machiavellian has a sporadic personality. They show duplicitous behaviors depending upon what they need from others or who they are talking with. You can find them completely different persons in every new day according to the situations and circumstances. It is better to give an example of politicians to make you aware of duplicity.

Tactical people:

They better know how to get methodical with their manipulation techniques. They are incredibly tactical to achieve their goals.

Charming indeed:

They know how to grab attention and generate trust. They choose the bunch of so many rights from dressing, facial and body expressions, tone, and words to obsess people with their charming personality. All these qualities make them master manipulator also.

Intimate toxic:

They can bring so much negativity and noxious in anyone's life. Their presence generates a feeling of being heavy and overwhelmed. They simply suppress the whole environment around them due to their toxicity.

All's well that ends well:

They just don't believe in ethics, morals, and rules. The only rule they follow is manipulation. They carry themselves in a very utilitarian way and feel free to do whatever they can to get favorable results. Philosophically they believe in "all's well that ends well".

Extremely narcissist:

Machiavellians always look for their interests and try to fix their problems and own paths of life. They never show any kind of magnanimity, amplitude, and conscientiousness for others.

Signs of psychopathic tendencies:

Machiavellians may suffer from mental illness of any kind that leads them only towards distraction. They may be only having the desire to destroy and ruin the lives of people around them only to calm down their evil deeds.

Try to get ahead:

The only result they expect is an ultimate success. They continuously work to get ahead of everyone, and for this, they follow no rules and ethics at all.

Narcissism

Narcissism is a normal element of child development, but after puberty, it is considered a disorder. This is a psychological disorder first identified in 1898 by Havelock Ellis. It is named for the mythological figure Narcissus, a character that fell in love with his reflection.

"Narcissism is an obsessive self-absorption characterized by fantasy addiction, abnormal self-possession and coolness, and an inflated self-image. It generates a tendency in narcissists to exploit abuse and take others for granted. A Narcissist thrives off everyone's attention and loathes simultaneously." Infants and small children are selfish, and they just want everything that they need or like. Children can't understand the desires and needs of others, but it is a normal part of child development. Similarly, in the teenager, every child becomes a little self-centered and wishes to get complete independence. But gradually these all habits get replaced by care, sincerity, and empathy.

When a growing teen shows unusual arrogance, limitless selfimportance, exaggeration about their success, popularity, and accomplishment......it is alarming. They exploit others for their gains, take advantage of people to feed their ego, and always remain in need of excessive admiration. They want to get power and desire to rule others. For this, they can divide people or pit them against each other. They present alternative facts and manipulate people by prompt emotions such as threatening, anger, and lies.

Signs Of Narcissism:

The diagnosis of Narcissism is not rocket science. No physical MRIs or blood tests are requiring determining Narcissism. You can implement a simple duck test-that is, if something looks like a duck and also quacks, it probably is a duck.

Simple observation of behaviors, reactions, and attitudes presented by a person are enough to determine Narcissism. Here is a descriptive list of signs and symptoms to identify Narcissism.

Validation and constant attention:

Narcissists don't believe that anyone can love them, and they feel very insecure and fearful. They always remain in constant need for praise from the people around them. The love, admiration, care, time, and validation you give to them always remains insufficient. They always remain in seek of more and more validation and attention, no matter how much you give them.

Need for control:

Narcissists always design a situation in their mind, prepare the arguments, and suggest the answers also. But when in reality, it doesn't happen similarly, they get disappointed and sad. They remain sad and disappointed with the unexpected and imperfect unfolds of life, but they want and demand to control every happening of their life.

Lack of communicating abilities:

Every kind of relationship requires understanding, cooperation, and thoughtfulness. It is equally important to realize the emotions, feelings, and sentiments of other persons involved in a relation. But Narcissists cannot realize the importance of duality in a relationship. They always act, behave, and understand according to their perceptions.

No guilty feelings:

The narcissist always considers himself on the right side of the argument. The narcissist always presents a false-self or pretends self-esteem. She/he always feels wrong or bad about you and never ashamed of her/himself. She/he always hides deficiencies, fears, rejections, and failures not only from others but from his/herself also.

Fear and anxiety:

Fears the alternate for their nature. They always remain chained up in an unseen fear. There is no particular reason for their fear, but they can even get scared or feared about germs, insult, shame, death, and feeling gratitude. As their relationships grow deep and closer, the more they feel scared, and the less they trust.

Fear creates anxiety. Narcissists not only experience anxiety and depression, but they try to transfer this to others. The more their closer ones feel worse, the narcissists feel better. They accuse or blame their loved ones and friends of behaving unsupportive, selfish, mentally ill, and not responsive to their needs.

· SPLITTERS:

Narcissists split everything and relationship into good and bad. For any positivity and goodness, they take credit for and leave

96

the opposite side for their closed ones. They continuously blame others for disapproving them but never accept their mistakes and always justify their negative words and actions. They cannot see the grey line between black and white and cannot able to mix the two constructs.

Perfectionism and superiority:

A narcissist considers him/her self at the top of the hierarchy, and only there feels safe. The whole world of a narcissist is categorized in the right/wrong, true/false, good/bad, and gentle/evil. A narcissist considers himself/herself the perfect, the most right, highly competent, and controls everyone, does everything in his way, and believes in being the best.

They only need to be on the top and can feel the superiority by being worse also. They reward themselves of being entitled to rights to hurt and manipulate people, receiving appease concerns, and right to hurt everyone. They don't request an apology, but they demand it and remain sure to get it in any way.

The greed of perfectionism:

For a narcissist, life is all about perfectionism. They contemplate their personality perfectly and consider every person, event, and thing that should be perfect. They want life to play out precisely according to their visualization. This desire for perfectionism leads them to depression, dissatisfaction, and anxiety.

Psychopath

Hervey Cleckley, in 1941 described Psychopathy as a disorder and separated it from "sociopath". The terms psychopath and sociopath are not officially available in official handbooks and generals of mental health. These two conditions are officially termed as "antisocial personality disorder".

"Psychopathy is an antisocial mental disorder in which a person exhibits antisocial and unprincipled behavior. A psychopath shows a lack of meaningful relationships, demonstrates an unsuccessful attempt to learn from it, shows having no ability to love, and expresses extreme self-centeredness. A Psychopath is not able to feel emotions like normal people."

The basic difference between psychopath and sociopath is the presence or absence of conscience. A psychopath does not have a conscience. That is why he won't understand any moral apprehension. Psychopaths are skilled actors. They are intelligent, smart, and pretty good in pretending and mimicking emotions. They are experienced enough to reach on the top of the corporate ladder, and they can even hurt others to reach there. They are cold-hearted, and at their worst, they have calculated killers also.

Signs of Psychopathy:

Although psychopathy considered a mental disorder, there is no known treatment for this kind of mental illness. A research conducted in 2010 reveals that only 1 out of 5 people with an antisocial personality disorder is a psychopath. There is a list of traits and signs of psychopathy:

- Pathological lying
- Escalated sense of self-worth
- The constant desire for energizing
- Lack of repentance or guilt
- Out of control behavior
- Insubstantial emotions
- Profligate sexual behavior
- Lack of long-term planning
- Unrealistic attitude
- Many marital relationships
- Irresponsibility
- Impulsiveness
- Criminal versatility
- Manipulative and conning others
- Believe in the blame game
- Lack of empathy

Chapter 12 Dark Persuasion Vs. Positive Persuasion

The distinction between persuasion and dark persuasion is the intention behind each activity. A persuasive person may be convincing another person to do something without having to think of the tactics to use or having a motivation. Dark persuaders, on the other hand, understand their intentions and have a bigger picture behind what they are doing. They know their victims and what motivates them to apply some tactics in persuading them.

Common Dark Persuasion Tactics

There are nine common techniques that dark persuaders use to persuade their victims successfully. The persuaders are well aware of their victims and will tactfully apply the methods to get what they want.

Foot in the Door

This is more of a principle that many dark persuaders follow. They ask their victims for smaller favors before asking for bigger favors. They first ask you for something little favor that will make you committed to helping them. The persuader then continues to ask for something bigger, which will be a way of continuing with something you had technically agreed on. Dark persuaders are aware that asking for small favor will increase your chances of agreeing to more prominent support.

Door in the Face Technique

Dark persuaders use the tactic in a quite different way from the foot in the door tactic. In this case, the persuader starts by requesting a bigger favor, and when you refuse, they do smaller favor. They are sure that refusing a bigger request increases your chances of accepting a smaller request. This technique of dark persuasion can be, for instance, be seen in people who work in sales. They request to purchase some things and when you decline they persuade you to buy at least one. You will likely feel it is not right to reject both requests and end up purchasing one of the products.

Anchoring

Dark persuaders use the technique to influence the decisions you are about to make. You can be a victim of dark persuasion in instances when you are purchasing a product. To determine its value, you can compare its price to a similar product and decide from there. Anchoring is a very powerful technique used by salespeople to persuade their customers to buy a product. For instance, when looking to buy a new motorbike and come across a good deal for 13000$. You bargain with the salesperson, and they agree to lower the cost to 10000$. You will go home feeling satisfied, and contempt is thinking of how well you bargained. However, it is possible the value of the motorbike was even lower than 10000$, and the initial price of 13000$ acted as an anchor to persuade you to purchase it. You end up getting convinced that anything lower than the initial price is a good deal.

Commitment and Consistency

Dark persuaders believe that people will always remain consistent in their beliefs and actions. They are sure that making a victim be committed to a small request increases the chances of using the first commitment to influencing them to do more. They do this by first asking you whether you support a certain deal. When you agree, they will make another request that will make you feel obliged to act on it because you showed your commitment.

Authority

Habitual dark persuaders focus on authority in any subject or field. They make their victims feel they are a source of authority. They act superior to coerce other people to do as they want for their benefits. For instance, a person who has a twitter handle and would like to gain more followers, they may convince people of how rich they are and make them follow them to learn the tactics of getting rich.

Social Proof

Dark persuaders have a way of making other people fall into their traps through social proof. They do this by making their car feel that everyone else believes or acts in a certain way, so should they. They make their victims do as their peers are doing. A real-life example is when going through Facebook posts, and you are more likely to add a like to post with many likes other than then one that has no likes and comments. A student can also fall victim to dark persuasion by being persuaded to smoke because everyone else in the class smokes.

Scarcity and Demand

This is one of the most commonly used technique by dark persuaders. Salespeople and marketers are habitual users of this technique to persuade people to buy their products. They use the scarcity technique as a target for people who prefer purchasing goods that are in low supply. They will convince a customer that the particular product is available for some limited time or its supply is very low. This increases their chances of liking and purchasing it. On the other hand, they use the demand tactic to convince people that the product is original and that everyone else is purchasing it. This way, a customer will feel convinced to buy the product. Dark persuaders using this technique have a motive of benefiting themselves and the company and not necessarily for the benefit of the customers.

Reciprocation

Human beings will always feel the obligation of returning favors. Dark persuaders are aware that people will always give something in return regardless of whether it will be pleasing. Dark persuasion involves making a victim indebted to them. They consistently make statements or act in a way that increases the chances of the victim, giving them something they need in return. An example is when a salesperson dealing with oranges gives a piece of orange for a customer to taste. The customer will feel indebted and end up purchasing then oranges even when they did not intend to.

Consensus

Dark persuaders believe in an old saying that there is safety in numbers. They apply the principle of consensus by making victims who are unsure of how to respond to some situations look at them and act as they act. The persuaders will convince a victim of making a certain choice by making them see there is no way all the other people who made a choice could be wrong. They make people feel motivated to move with the crowd with the sense that there is some safety in numbers. For instance, a hotel where customers are persuaded to reuse their towels. The customers are convinced that reusing the towels is an environmental benefit and that most people who check-in the hotel does so. This increases the chances of the customers reusing the towels even when they are unsure about it.

Dark Seduction

Dark seduction involves the use of coercive and manipulative techniques to get other people like you. There are various techniques used in dark seduction. These include;

Choosing the Right Victim

The art of dark seduction is dependent on the seduction target. Dark seducers tend to thoroughly study their prey and select those that seem much susceptible to their seduction charms.

They tend to go for victims who seem unhappy, antisocial, and isolated. Choosing a perfect victim makes it easier for the seducers to have a smooth chase.

Creating a False Sense of Security

Approaching Indirectly- Dark seducers tactfully approach their targets because when they do it directly, their motives will not be fulfilled. They consider approaching a target at an angle that makes them eventually know who they are. They focus on coming up with a neutral relationship gradually moving from a mutual friend to becoming a lover. They instill some feelings of security to the target and finally strike their motives.

Sending Mixed Signals

Dark seducers have a way of making people recognize their presence and intrigue their attention before it shifts to other people. They send some mixed reactions such as earthly and spiritual, innocent and cunning, as well as tough and tender. These signals make people be drawn to them easily as they seek to know more about them. Dark seducers ensure they have created a power that hints something not really within them.

Appearing to be an Object of Desire

Creating Triangles- Dark seducers follow the analogy that people will always be attracted to those who have attracted the interest of others. To draw their victims closer, dark seducers make people hunger for their possession. People will be enticed to act in the best possible way to become the center of attention.

They do this to try and win the dark seducer from the group of admirers.

Creating a Need

Stirring Anxiety and Discontent- As a satisfied person, you cannot easily fall into the traps of dark seducers. This is because dark seducers tend to instill disharmony and tension in their targets. They instill in them feelings of unhappiness and discontent in the circumstances they are in. The kind of inadequacy created in the victims makes them feel that the seducer is the only solution to the problems they are experiencing. Dark seducers will always study their target carefully to determine the need that they can fill.

Mastering the Art of Insinuation

Dark seduction involves making a victim feel dissatisfied and that the seducer's attention is all they require. They do this by making everything suggestive.

Creating Temptation

Luring the target deep into dark seduction involve coming up with a relative temptation. Dark seducers use some tactics that are beyond the control of the victim. They study their weaknesses, fantasies they are yet to realize and come up with a hint that will allow the victim to follow them. They ensure they have made the victim's curiosity stronger.

Isolating the Victim

Dark Seduction applies this technique in a bid to make the victim more vulnerable to the influence of the seducer. They do this by removing the victim from their normal home, family, friends, and colleagues. The victims start feeling marginalized for leaving the environment they are used to and entering another. They feel they lack outside support, and they can easily be led amiss.

Stirring up the Transgressive and Taboo

Dark Seducers know that many people are ready to explore the dark side of life. They will seduce such victims by convincing them they are being led beyond their limits. Once the target has the desire to transgress, it becomes difficult for them to stop. A powerful bond ends up being created between the seducer and the target.

Tips To Help You Avoid Being A Subject Of Dark Seduction

Be Alert

Always consider looking at your surroundings to establish the kind of people around you. Dark seducers are likely to identify their targets easily. Consider making brief eye contact with everyone around you, but do not stare at them. Try to avoid being scared, and do not keep on checking your phone.

Walk with Purpose

Dark seducers are likely to identify people who seem confused and make them their targets. Walk like you are aware of where you are going. In case you have to ask for directions, do not stop people on the streets but ask from store clerks, restaurant employees, or guards on shops or offices.

Do Not Allow People to Stop You

Dark seducers will do anything possible to make people fall into their traps. Do not be too easy to stop a stranger anytime asks you to. Just keep moving and do not follow strangers.

Closely Watch Your Body Language

Ensure you walk in an organized way. This is because dark seducers will target people who show fear and physical vulnerability as they walk.

Chapter 13 Dark Psychological Seduction

Seduction can be defined in several ways, depending on which angle you view it from. It may be sexual, which is the most common definition. In this case, a person is tempted to engage in sexual intercourse. Often, such an individual may be opposed to this act. A less common definition is, ironically, one that is seen everywhere and every time. It involves enticing an individual or groups of people with any particular offer, which may not be as true as presented.

Seduction, both of the sexual and non-sexual kind, is used in marketing with increasing frequency. This is especially noticeable in recent times. Sparsely clad male and female models are used for advertising anything from undergarments to toothbrushes. Hence the common saying that 'sex sells.' But this is not to hint that seduction is a modern concept. In fact, it dates many years in the past, even before Homo sapiens began to form societies. Seductive behaviors can be observed in various animals during their mating rituals. Don Juan is a popular fictional character, written as far back as the 1630s, who was infamous for womanizing. This would often involve seducing women of different types for his sexual gratification. To manipulate women into giving in to his advances, Don Juan might change his look. As such, he is depicted to be a shapeshifter; a cunning power associated with the devil. There is also the real-life story of Giacomo Casanova, whose unfettered licentiousness accounted, to some extent, for his infamy. Femme fatale, as it relates to seduction, is a word used to describe a particularly driven seductress. In the English language, it is translated to mean Deadly Woman. These women are usually beautiful and self-aware. They use their sexual appeal and seductive charm as a weapon to bend the will of those they have targeted and, in so doing, achieve their goals.

Other characteristics of the femme fatale are the blinding desire for survival, even to the detriment of their target of seduction. They may be selfish, cruel, single-minded, and determined. Some famous names, both in real life and fiction, in this category include Cleopatra, Lucrezia Borgia, Lilith, Lady Macbeth, Marie Antoinette of Austria, Morgan le Fay, and Salome.

The lack of empathy and manipulative devices utilized during seduction has been some of the reasons why seduction is associated with the dark triad, although these attributes are only observed in short-term seduction, as long-term would require more commitment.

TECHNIQUES OF SEDUCTION

There are a variety of ways but which a seducer may go about enticing anyone and getting them to act outside their will. The listed seduction techniques cut across both the sexual and nonsexual kind. They also include some popular methods of seduction and those that are more subtle.

Flattery: most people would detect this quickly and point it out to the seducer. But, if it is done subtly and the insecurities of the victim are taken into account, it just might go unnoticed. No one is without these insecurities. We all have, at least, one area in our lives where we feel inadequate and seek someone or something to validate us. Seducers who use flattery to get their way are quite observant and would prey on such weaknesses. They are often skilled at not being obvious, either with their choice of words or mannerisms. The reassurance they give to their victims is often very effective at gaining their trust. Sale marketers do not shy away from using flattery to convince their audience that a particular product is the best fit for them. Mirror: in this case, the seducer tries to show to his or her victim they are similar, whether it is in their experiences, beliefs, abilities, etc. This works because of the notion of compatibility. We are often moved to choose those people, as relationship partners, business partners, friends, and so on, who share some things in common with us. When you see something of yourself in someone else, you would likely be drawn to that individual. The seducer may lie to their victim about their interest in a particular genre of music, simply to get them to feel safe and relaxed. It is even more effective when the shared experience is a negative one. The seducer might talk about how they have also been heartbroken by a cheating partner, just to get their victim to feel a false connection or bond. Where else do we see such in play? If you guessed advertisements, then you are correct. We are told that a brand is as family-minded or as fun-seeking as we are. As such, we make that product brand our personal choice. Fantasy: we all have imaginations of what the perfect romantic partner would be. How they would behave towards us, the words they will say to us their sense of style, their goals, etc. The seducer, to execute their desire, may go out of their way to bring their victim's dreams and fantasies to life. They would get the needed information from studying their target or asking the person's close friends and family members. Then the seducer proceeds to become the victim's person of fantasy. They do the roses on the staircase, lights, music, and show interest in the victim's children if they have any, offer to fix certain things in the house, and so on. If done right, the victim, for that moment in time, feels like they have hit the jackpot. They are forthcoming with whatever is asked of them by the seducer. Some, especially dark individuals, may take this a bit further and derive some enjoyment from shattering the fantasy they had created. After all, it is all a game to them, and there were no actual emotions involved on their part.

Shaming: should the seducer not get their way; they might resort to guilt-tripping and shaming techniques. Unlike the method of flattery, where the seducer enforces the ego of their victims and makes them feel good, shaming does the opposite. The inadequacies and faults of the victim are brought to light, and they are made to believe that their choices or decisions would only lead to unfortunate results, whether in the near or far future. This works quite effectively on people with low selfesteem. At that point, they may be willing to do anything just to please their seducer and feel worthy again.

Logical fallacy: these are errors committed during arguments whereby the reasoning of a person arguing is faulty. It may be done deliberately or unintentionally to misdirect, confuse, or make an argument seem more solid and whole than it is. It is done quite often by seducers, especially when they are being resisted. For example, a seducer might pose that their victims would yield to their advances if they, indeed, loved them. This is not exactly accurate, as many unrelated factors could account for why a person may refuse to give in to any request, sexual or not. The seducer could also argue that denying their desires at that particular point in time may result in a domino effect, which would ultimately cause the end of the relationship. This is called the slippery slope fallacy and is one of the most common types. These fallacious arguments are often delivered with such conviction of tone and mannerisms that it appears true and factual.

False control of decision: have you been accosted by a salesperson who, after some minutes of telling you all you stand to gain and lose depending on your decision, still says, in the end, that it is still your choice to make? In truth, it is your choice to make. This false sense of control makes the person being seduced feel like they are in charge, even as they give in to the request of their seducer.

Minimizing: this is another common tactic used by seducers in the convincing of their targets. They try to make a situation that holds great importance seem trivial. They would say things like, "this is not such a big deal" (this involves a fallacy called hasty generalization), and "everyone does this" in an attempt to make their victims believe there is nothing to be wary of. They might also go further to minimize the fears of the individual being seduced, by telling them to worry and that it does not betray the seriousness of the situation whatsoever.

Vilification: usually, when someone is trying to manipulate another into doing something against their personal choices, it is the seducer who seems like the bad guy. But, to get their way, the seducer might turn this around on their victim and make them feel like the villain for saying no. If the victim is a neurotic or one who is a people-pleaser, this tactic would work quite well in getting them to give in to their seducers. The seducer would pretend to be hurt and act the victim. This would place the actual victim in the position of the villain. A role I'm which neurotics and people-pleasers are uncomfortable in.

Pretending to be innocent: this seduction technique bears some similarities to playing the victim, but it differs in that the actual victim is not vilified, and the seducer does not pretend to be hurt. Instead, the pretense is one of naivete, near cluelessness, and innocence. When it has to do with sex, they might tell their victims that they are virgins, and have only been keeping themselves for the right person. They make them appear unlike 'every other guy or girl' who only wants the victim for sex or some other type of material gain. The victim may also feel closer to their seducer if they are novices on the subject.

Seduction is a game that has been played throughout the ages, and one that continues to be a weapon in the arsenal of so many. The methods listed here are nothing new, but they expose the dark psychology at play during such manipulative activities.

Chapter 14 Case Studies

The mystery of dark psychology has baffled many and continues to be an element of shock and wonder. It is without a doubt this kind of depraved, twisted psychology that is the driving force behind serial killers and many baffling cases that defy the human conscience. That leaves us with a question - is the dark psychology a rare occurrence in some people, or we all susceptible to its depraved logic? That's a question for another day, though.

Below we look at some baffling cases that have prominently put to the fore the mystery of dark psychology. What we notice is that the worst of human traits, the darkness that lives in all of us, come out during experiments. And not just in the subjects. Even the ones experimenting showed great inhumanity.

Scientific Experiments

The scientist has conducted experiments on people for as long as science and experiments and hypotheses have existed. Yet, there was a strange twist. It was a twist, perhaps more twisted than the entire subversives of dark psychology. Scientists have also been in the fore in proving the dark psychology as they attempted to find out about something else. So traumatizing were these experiments that some of the participants' permanent psychological issues. Most of them involved manipulating test subjects to get them to perform, which you will realize as one of the dark personality traits - Machiavellian. In the 1960s, a doctor came to light after it emerged that she used electroshock therapy on children. The horror didn't start there, as, during the interview process, she would select her patients by having a parent bring their child, where she would press their heads. Any slight movement and she would declare the child had schizophrenia. And during the shock, she never showed sympathy on the children, with her youngest being just three years.

Then, from 53-73, the government of the US embarked on experiments that would help them find out how to manipulate people. The project was called MKUltra. These experiments involved subjecting people without their knowledge, to drugs that altered their brains, hypnosis, sexual abuse, and many other forms of torture. This experiment just gave a glimpse of the murk that was human psychology. Subjecting innocent people to such cruelty in the name of the research was itself peak dark psychology.

The most famous experiment in psychology was the Stanford Experiment, which aimed to find out the cause of conflict between the prisoners and their guards. The scientist selected twenty-four prisoners and assigned them roles of either guards or prisoners. Then they were awarded a model prison within the premises. What emerged was that the prisoners playing guards were so strict and so extreme in their torture of the prisoners that the scientists stopped the experiment after just six days!

Sick.

The Milgram experiment was also another that put to the fore the repressed terrible recesses of human psychology. In 1961, Stanley Milgram, a Yale University Psychologist, set out to find just why Eichmann and other millions of soldiers in the Holocaust just followed orders. This was a quarter a year after Eichmann had gone to trial. Two people were placed in separate rooms but could hear each other. The experiment was to see the willingness of someone to follow authority orders. Between these two participants, one was an actor. The test subject would then read the question to the actor, and if the actor answered any of them wrongly, the test subject would administer an electric shock to the actor. Nearly every single test subject continued pressing the electric shock button when the experimenter to them that they would not be held personally responsible for their actions.

Another case was of David Peter Reimer, who was born biologically male. When he was just seven months, he suffered a damaging injury to his manhood as someone circumcised him. John Money, a psychologist and a great believer in gender as something that one learns, convinced David's parents that their son would more likely be more functional as a girl. He must have been a Machiavellian. But while Money put his money on his idea is a success, David's account much contradicted Money's. David never identified as female, so that is where it all falls apart. David spent his childhood traumatized due to being teased and ostracized, leaving him depressed. Then, at just 38 years old, David couldn't take it anymore and committed suicide with a gunshot to the head.

Another example of the scientists being total monsters was in the Washington and Oregon prison testicle radiation experiment. Between 1963 and 1973, several inmates from these two prisons volunteered as test subjects in a trial that aimed to find the effects of radiation on testicles. One hundred thirty inmates were bribed with cash and promise of parole to take part in the experiment. Here, we see the dark part of the scientist come out. Manipulating prisoners into taking part in a dangerous operation is inhumane. The inmates agreed to take part in the experiment. The study was the brainchild of the government.

The scientists exposed some of the test subjects to massive doses of radiation. Now, exposure to radiation is dangerous, even when it is in small doses. Radiation rays have a permanent effect on the human cells, mutating the DNA and other cells in the body, leading to deformities. This affects not just the test subject, but the children will have as well. It was only much later that the prisoners found out that they had not been told about the whole truth regarding the dangers of the experiment. They settled a $2.4 million agreement at the turn of the century.

Psychopaths - Serial Killers

Serial killers have, for a long time, held the fascination of many people. Their wanton disregard for necessary human conscience has forever baffled and intrigued not just the ordinary people, but the figures of authority, scientists, and psychologists. One of the many questions that one finds themselves asking when watching a serial killer documentary is - are we responsible beings, or would we become them if we felt like we would not be held to book? If we had nothing to lose, would we be just as lethal? If the Milgram experiment above was anything to go by, perhaps we could be just as prone to violence as serial killers. But still, the lack of inhibition shown by these killers is legendary, a revelation of the darkness rolling just beneath our human conscience.

Ed Gein was a farmer in Plainfield, Wisconsin, notorious for robbing women's bodies from graves. He also was a murderer and often used parts of the women's remains to decorate his isolated farm in Wisconsin and make items on clothing. Gein was active between 1945-1957 and died in 1984 at a mental institution. He had so much impact that he was loosely used to create fictional killers.

Night Stalker

Richard Ramirez was a deranged murderer that came to be dubbed by the media as 'The Night Stalker.' In 14 months, Ramirez embraced the night as his accomplice, gravitating towards the embrace of the dark as he made a way through homes in a prowl that saw him leave behind 13 dead across California.

Before he made his first kill, the authority had arrested Ramirez for attempted rape, but the woman did not pursue the case, choosing not to testify against him. Let, free, Ramirez began a long murder spree that was violent, brutal, and callous. He often showed no remorse, and his first murder victim, 76-year old Jennie Vincow, on June 28th, 1984. Ramirez brutally raped then murdered the woman by slitting the throat so deep that she was almost decapitated.

During his trial, he gave little away in terms of remorse, and as he was led to prison to serve his life sentence. On his way to prison, he couldn't help but taunt the people gathered outside the court to witness his trial.

Ramirez had a difficult childhood, suffering two severe head injuries that left him suffering from frequent epileptic attacks. His father was abusive to him, leading to Ramirez running away from home. He found comfort in his cousin Miguel, a war veteran, who had developed a taste for torturing women in Vietnam. He showed Ramirez the photos of the torture and killed his wife as Ramirez watched. Miguel may have influenced Ramirez to develop a taste for blood.

Grim Sleeper

When women began disappearing at a neighborhood in Los Angeles, no one would have suspected the personable Loonie Frankline Jr. Neighbors and friends described him as someone willing to help and didn't display the usual traits of psychopathy, like being a loner.

Franklin earned his nickname due to the 14-year break he seemed to have taken between murdering his first eight victims between 1985-1988. He began again in 2002, though authorities believe that he may be responsible for more deaths than the eleven the court found him guilty of.

Franklin targeted women and with hundreds of polaroid photos of women, some of whom were his victims, others who were still alive. Others were never identified, which led authorities to suspect him of more deaths than what he was charged with. Franklin shot his victims at close range and dumped them near trash cans and on alleyways. Often, he would target vulnerable women off the streets.

He was sentenced to death in August 2016, although authorities are still trying to connect him to 15 other killings.

Edmund Kemper

Kemper was a bright child who suffered a lot of abuse, physical and emotional, under his mother. He had also been displaying psychopathic tendencies as a child, often torturing and killing animals, which is observed in a big number of people who end up being psychotic killers.

He often decapitated his sister's dolls as a child and had once stalked his teacher in second grade outside her home with his father's bayonet. When he was ten, Kemper killed the family's cat. Then, he killed another when he was 13. This second time, he took up some parts of the animal and kept them in the cloth closet, where his mother came across them, much to her horror probably.

When he was 14, he left home to find his father in California. His determination to see his old man paid off, but rather than find comfort and the man rejected him. He had been belittled continuously by Kemper's mother, and this may have led him to hate the boy. Depressed and angry, he went to live with his grandparents, both of whom he shot dead in 1964, at just 15. He was then committed to Atascadero State Hospital for the criminally insane but was released back to his mother five years later, much to his chagrin.

He began fantasizing about killing his mother but decided first to perfect his murder skills.

Between 1972 and 1973, Kemper began his killing spree. Targeting female students, he would pick up those hitchhiking a ride on the road. But then, rather than take them to their destination, he took them out in the wild, where he killed them. Then, to further add to his derangement, he would have sex with the dead women, decapitate them and take their heads back to his apartment, where he would have sex with them too. Scary stuff this one.

Then, in 1973, on Good Friday, Kemper achieved what may have been his biggest goal—he murdered his mother. Taking a hammer, he bludgeoned her to death, then proceeded to strangle her friend. Afterward, he also defiled his mother's head.

After he was done, he made a phone call to the local police, where he confessed to them. They were initially reluctant to arrest him, as he was known to them, but they were down on him soon after he began revealing details of the murders that only the murderer would know. At this point, when they came to take him, he did not resist. He was just twenty-four at the time.

Alton Coleman And Debra Brown

The Bonnie and Clyde of the serial killer's horrific world, the two traversed across six states, leaving eight people dead in their wake.

At age 19, Coleman had already had six counts of rape charged against him. It was reported that Coleman had unusually strong sexual urges that he then took to satisfying with all people, including children.

In May 1984, he befriended Juanita White, a single mother of two children, 14-year old Vernita White, and her younger brother. After befriending Juanita over a few weeks, he then asked for permission from Juanita to have Vernita accompany him to his house to pick up a stereo system on May 29th. Both never came back, and Vernita was found brutally murdered, raped, and bound with a TV cord.

Then, in the company of Debra, his girlfriend, they abducted two children, Tamika, and Annie as they walked and left school for home. The two were very young, seven and nine, respectively.

The two depraved beings then tied up the children, and when Tamika couldn't stop crying, Debra covered her mouth while Coleman, without remorse, stepped on her chest. But they were not done. They killed her by strangulation, then both defiled Annie beat her and choked her, but Annie lived through the ordeal.

Then, on the same day, they abducted Donna Williams, from Indiana, who had known Coleman for a few weeks. She was found on July 11th, 1984. She had been strangled, and her car was close by. What this even scarier was that the incident took place just a short distance from Coleman's grandma's house. Then, they were in Ohio four days later, where they gained the trust of another African American family, headed by Virginia Temple. Temple had three children, with Rachelle, 9, being the oldest. The pair strangled Virginia and Rachelle and then put their bodies in the crawlspace in the home's basement. The other two children were not harmed, and Virginia's mother found them when she came to visit.

Theirs was also merely a murder seemingly for the thrill of it, an indictment into the twist of human psychology when you dig deep.

According to Del Paulhus, a personality psychologist, the four dark personalities - Machiavellian, Narcissism, Psychopathy and Sadism, these personalities are fascinating than the typical personality types, which could explain our obsession with serial killers and their actions of extreme, often without any apparent motive.

Del Paulhus called for more linking between these dark personalities typed, despite their distinct concepts.

Looking at it, you get the sense that, indeed, they are part of the same basic structure. All four personality types often will be reflective of the doers' view of the world. To kill, you will need a set of distinguishing traits, after all, to begin to murder, then keep murdering, and with increasing violence and seeming glee. On their own, these cases of call for us to give more attention to what precisely the dark psychology is and how we can look into it further. Beneath our human conscience, lies a dark underworld, waiting for just the right trigger to come to the fore.

Chapter 15 Our Dark Side

Have you ever thought of creating a negative impact on this life? Sometimes people are engrossed with the right things or morals they have and forget their dark sides. Other scenarios are where one is prized highly even by parents that you value yourself of a higher standard than your counterparts. That feeling is sometimes unfortunate because you may think you are right in anything, whereas other individuals see our weakness. That is why it is good to accept all corrections as one cannot identify their ills or wrongs unless you are told.

What about the dark side you have? You may be surprised to know that the dark side in you can be used as an advantage. Sometimes one is too proud to recognize the vices one has. Other people know their vices, and they feel pressured to control them, therefore generating a personality disorder. You may be that guy who is always viewed to be wicked; thus, everybody fears that character in you. You, therefore, feel isolated and think you cannot do anything to change their perception of you. Another instance is that you may have been involved in a sorrowful ordeal. Your past tends to determine the life course one chooses. You feel that you cannot try a particular task because you failed once, and you believe you are a complete failure. Maybe at one time, you were short-tempered to the extent of injuring your friend or sibling with a machete. Therefore, you will grow with the attitude that there is a hidden darkness in you.

In some cases, this is the demonic part of you, and you should try to control it in every way. Many relationships have broken because the partners did not take time to know the evil of the other. All they shared is their bright linen, and they did not take time to understand the dirty linen of the other spouse. It would be hurting to know the prince charming or the queen you once believed can hart you in a way you never expected.

Therefore, it is suitable for everybody to recognize the demonic part of you and try to share it with anyone who can understand. Moreover, before getting into a relationship, dig in the background to identify the weakness of your beloved.

Everybody has the evil spirit inside, which you may know or do not. Do you ever think your enemies can ever tell you something positive? But consider asking them what they hate you for, you may realize they do not hate you but dislikes the vice in you. You may further be surprised that they want you to change for the better. It is essential to know who your real friends are because some are fake friends. They will relate with you to discover your weakness, of which they will exploit you negatively.

Having that evil side is sometimes a positive thing because you will know your true nature. Sometimes you are afraid that your close friend will discover your dark side and laugh at you. At other times you like living alone because you feel the demon in you will harm the people you care. Such people experience low self-esteem and do not see any value in themselves. However, there is good news. do you know even the best of you may be the dark side to other people? You may be that bright guy in school or that star player, but do you know too much of anything is poisonous. You are used to being praised or celebrated by your colleagues; therefore, you developed that arrogance attitude. Hence that is an evil nature in you.

How Can One Use the Evil Nature in You for Your Advantage? You use that character one has to know who your real friends are. The worst betrayal is that which comes from close friends. That pal of yours may not even love you but as waiting at that moment you. Sometimes these friends are interested in the possessions or the richness you have, but when poverty strikes you, they will eclipse. Kings or queens are followed because of the influence, wealth, and authority they commission to that kingdom, but not out of the love the subjects have for them. Your dark nature in you will disconnect you from fake friends and connect you to real allies.

This feeling helps one to have an attitude of self-acceptance. Maybe you have done everything to stop these evils. However, your hustles are fruitless. You eventually feel that it is an epidemic that you cannot fight. However, by realizing your true nature, you will consequently learn that attitude to accept yourself. Therefore, you can face people confidentially as you feel you have the power to control that evilness you have. Being weak and feeling disoriented in society is another negative impact of the dark side of you. However, if you learn to manage those feelings, you will have no more fear to face society. You will undoubtedly identify those people who are ready to support you and finish that distrust you possess. Sometimes you may have done wrong that you fear to repeat such actions. Consequently, you even fear yourself, but if you do selfevaluation, you will stop that attitude.

Sometimes the evilness in you can help you to attain you want. You can be dictatorial in any way, but that attitude will command respect and obedience from your subordinates. They will fear you and will try to do everything right to please you. You always have a negative attitude in everything, but you will be a winner if your optimistic friend loses in an area, he thought was achievable. If people fear that you will hurt them, they will allow you to do everything that pleases you.

Some scholars say that you can only 'solve evil with evil.' This ideology works when one wants to reduce the vices found in society. You are that saint whom everybody respects, but how can you fight those criminals who fight you if you do not know how they think. Therefore, if you have a Dark side, you will learn about it and recognize how to deal with it. Therefore, if your counterpart has the same element, you will be in a position to manage him. That is why most people use reformed addicts or criminals to advise other individuals suffering under the same umbrella.

How Can One Use the Dark Side To Manipulate People? Many are the cases people are conned, and they often say that the culprit manipulated them. This move can go to an extent where a person is coerced or brainwashed to do something of, not their wish. Manipulation in some people can be viewed as a vice that is not acceptable. It is usually a way of influencing, coercing, or persuading a person to agree with what you want. In this case, you are the dominant force, and your counterpart is the less dominant person. Many of the manipulators use different approaches in eliciting you to do what they want. Some may be sweet-talking to influence you to do something that even you did not wish to. Others will forcefully blackmail you or corer you to do a favor,

Manipulation is an example of the dark side that you may possess. Being manipulated sometimes shows that you are gullible, and you can easily be fooled to do something that you never wished. Those particular people who influence others are mostly emotionally intelligent guys. Such personnel play around with your feelings, and you sense danger you do not follow their instructions. One may ask how the dark nature in you is connected to manipulation. Remember that manipulation may be positive or negative, but in this case, consider manipulation on positive grounds. If you are a parent, you must show you the wrong side so that the children can obey you. Imagine how you feared to do wrong when you were a kid because you were afraid of caning from parents. Therefore, the parents will manipulate you in doing something right by using such painful measures.

Isn't that the right side of manipulation prompted by the dark side?

What are Yin and Yang

It is a Chinese philosophy that shows how contrary parties or opposite ones may intermingle, connect, and interdepend on each other. You will always feel oriented to mingle with another even if you do not share the same class. This principality is associated with the dark nature one has. Yin is expressed and marked as evil, wicked, feminist, and shadows. While Yang is marked as bright, masculinity, heaven, and eminence, these two groups of people usually relate to energize their colleague. Recognize that Yang is mostly associated with males, and Yin is associated with females.

It has been found that both of these qualities very different and are used in manipulation. A Yin person is characterized by being a listener, softy, coolness, surrender, and respectful. In Yang people, they are portrayed in being brave, authoritative, and strict. Therefore, in most cases, the Yang People Influences the

Yin individuals

Ten Ways Manipulators Use Their Dark Sides

Manipulators mostly cheat to gain an advantage over you. The specific issues that they mainly cheat is to generate pity from you. They will lie about a particular episode that happened to them, and they will try to connect that story on what they aim you to perform. Therefore, you will feel motivated by what they want to do to prevent such a terrible episode from happening to you. Think of a person who tells you not to walk on a particular street because burglars attacked him. You will surely not walk on that path. Therefore, without knowing the person will influence you to walk on the road, he or she wants. They mostly instill your fear. These individuals like warning their victims, which is a way of instilling phobia on doing something you are meant to do. For the case of that street, they scare you like 'burglars will attack you if you follow the same path I followed.' It is the nature of a being to fear the danger or horrifying scenes. Therefore, they use such a weakness of people to their advantage. They may even fake a story or use an illustration of the sad story of a person who followed the path they do not want you to take. You will undoubtedly try to avoid such episodes, and hence you will fall in their trap. These people can identify when you're happy and take advantage of that situation. Happiness is a good thing for every human, which one aims to have. Every activity that one does or practices the most significant priority is to achieve maximum happiness. They can do soothing that will make you jovial as a way of capturing your attention. Whenever you are in discussion with them, they will jump to that topic, which they perceive is interesting to you. You will undoubtedly hear them out after you realize they focus on things that entice you. Without knowing they will use that chance to influence to fulfill their wishes.

Imagine hearing a person singing the song you like; you will undoubtedly stop what you are doing to hear them out. Manipulators always like blackmailing their victims. That is where they use the reciprocity rule when engaging you. This rule states that do unto others as they have done for you. If maybe you are in a job interviewing panel, and you realize someone buys you some presents before the interview. Know that the particular person wants to manipulate you to favor him in job recruitment. What if you take their valuable gifts which you cannot afford to compensate them, you will only be left with one choice, which is that you will have to favor them. Therefore, if you realize such people, please do not accept their presents or gifts.

These folks always want to be the center of the conversation. They like painting a picture that they know much from you. Even when you are conversing with them, they will try to put much vocabulary and jargon to make you look inferior. By doing this, you will develop the fear of criticizing them and correcting them. They always seek influence and dominates amid the conversation you have. You can even create an attitude that they know better than you, hence everything they say you will find it right and intelligent. The route they want you to follow, you will undoubtedly observe that path. To manage such people, it is essential to have a neutral talk where all of you have the same say. Whenever you feel that they are trying to gain dominance, cut the story off, and remind them that you share the same grounds.

These persons always ask lots of questions. They ask such questions when they give you less space to answer. You will realize that they still talk to fast that you cannot easily comprehend what they are saying. Hey, that is a scheme they develop to hide their real intention. The questions will be based on your failures, where they want to discover such weaknesses to blackmail you. They want to talk fast so that they can blame you that you are the one not listening well. Allowing you to criticize them or correct them will expose evil schemes, which is something they would not love.

These people always want you to look like the villain in any terrible story. They want you to feel like you are the guilty one in any situation. They will cite an episode you were involved in and try to show you that you are the one who made a mistake. They use such a weapon because they know that it is human nature to try to justify themselves. Therefore, they give you a platform to excuse yourself from an ordeal where they place their demands as a means of that justification. Therefore, you will surely do what they want to remove your dirty linen out of the public sight.

Showing their negative emotions is one way to trick you into doing what they require. They may even fake a sentiment that will touch you. They can feign anger, sorrowfulness, remorse, and other emotions. Remember, they want to gain control of your feelings. Imagine how what would you do if your beloved kid threatens to kill himself if you do not buy him the promise. You will surely be manipulated to buy him that toy, where the kid was faking that emotion as it is impossible for the child to kill himself.

Sometimes these individuals want to show you that they are favoring you more than others. Whenever they award you with something, they will whisper how they preferred you in that situation. They will tell you that you have impressed them in a certain way, and they feel obliged to return the favor. They want you to look superior over others, as is the nature of a person to feel praised above others. Therefore, you will be enticed to do what they want so that they can keep on complementing you often.

Conclusion

Thank you for making it through to the end!

The next step is to make the best use of your new-found wisdom of Dark Psychology and protect yourself and your loved ones from being a victim at the hands of predators using their Dark Psychology to their advantage. Take a step back and reassess the negative influences in your life. You have now armed yourself to fight them back with your knowledge and understanding of the Dark Psychology and its various modes of manifestation. You have also learned how NLP can help you transform your weaknesses and insecurities into positive affirmations and increasing confidence. Mastering the art of persuasion will allow you to improve your loved ones into making better life decisions. With your renewed understanding of the difference between belief and dark manipulation, you can quickly identify your friends from your enemies. Remember, with high power, comes get responsibility. So, exercise caution while using your new psychological powers.

CPSIA information can be obtained
at www.ICGtesting.com
Printed in the USA
LVHW011014140121
676458LV00010B/293